B2B Account Management

Bill Senese

Copyright © 2025 Willnata LLC

www.willnata.com

Denver, CO

All rights reserved.

No part of this publication may be reproduced, distributed, or transmitted in any form or by any means, including photocopying, recording, or other electronic or mechanical methods, without the prior written permission of the publisher, except as permitted by U.S. copyright law. For permission requests, contact: admin@willnata.com.

The information in this publication is for educational and informational purposes only. It is not intended to be a substitute for professional advice. Willnata LLC is not responsible for any actions taken based on the information provided.

Cover Design by Bill Senese

Library of Congress Control Number: 2025916628

First edition 2025

ISBN: 979-8-9927726-3-0

To the account managers who helped me learn when I knew nothing, and to those reading now with the same drive to grow. May this book be the guide I once needed, and the edge you've been looking for.

CONTENTS

	Prologue: A Day in the Life	i
1	What is B2B Account Management?	1
2	The Skills That Set You Apart	16
3	Email Communication	29
4	Verbal Communication	51
5	In-Person Meetings	61
6	One-to-One and Small Group Meetings	74
7	One-to-Many Meetings	90
8	Virtual Meetings	104
9	Listening and Responding	119
10	Relationship Building	133
11	Customer Obsession	145
12	Presentation Building	158
13	Presenting, Pitching, and Selling	173
14	Follow-Up and Follow-Through	187
15	Flexibility and Creativity	203
16	Rapid Learning and Resourcefulness	217
17	Understanding and Using Metrics	229
18	Putting it All Together	240
	Glossary of Account Management Terms	251

Prologue:

A Day in the Life

It's 7:18 a.m. You're halfway through your first cup of coffee, scanning emails on your phone, when one subject line grabs you: "Escalation – PO 78459 Late Again."

Before you've finished reading, your phone buzzes, it's your manager, copied on the email, asking if you've seen it. You send a quick reply letting them know you are on top of it and flag the email so you can come back to it later.

By 8:15, you're on your first internal call of the day, a team sync with your manager and peers. You share updates on a few accounts, talk through some open deals, and learn about a new feature launching this week. One of your customers has been asking for that exact capability. You jot a note and fire off a quick email while the call's still going.

At 9:00, you're in a virtual meeting with a long-time customer, pitching an expansion you've been working on for weeks. The presentation lands well, but they're not ready to move. You thank them for the feedback and, before you even close Zoom, start drafting your follow-up.

As soon as the call ends, you're back in your inbox. A note from your largest customer catches your eye. They want to meet in person. They're across the country, so you check your calendar, send availability, and block time to build a deck. Before you can breathe, your next meeting is five minutes away.

At 10:30, you join a one-to-one with another customer. There's no formal agenda; you're relationship-building, planting seeds for future growth. They casually mention an upcoming acquisition and that they need support bringing the new unit into their account. You flag it as a potential expansion opportunity.

The moment you hang up, a teammate pings you: *"Hey, how'd you handle that pricing objection from last week?"* You share your approach and jump back to email.

At 11:30, a calendar reminder hits; it's time to finalize the deck for a training session later today. You'd prepped most of it last week, but you tweak a few slides and tighten the flow.

At noon, you scarf lunch while watching a mandatory cybersecurity training corporate's been chasing you on. It's dry, but if you don't finish it, you'll lose network access.

By 1:00, you're deep into QBR prep for your largest customer. You're reviewing metrics, shaping the narrative, and rehearsing how to connect the data to the outcomes they care about.

At 2:00, you're back on a virtual call, this time on Teams, with the top buyer at one of your smaller accounts. They drop a curveball: they've been promoted, and a new buyer is taking over next week. You smile, congratulate them, and immediately ask to be introduced to their replacement. Relationship continuity just became your top priority.

At 2:45, your 3:00 customer cancels at the last minute. You use the opening to scan account trends and spot two red flags. One has dropping revenue; the other shows a spike in support tickets. You send an email to one requesting a meeting and add the other to tomorrow's priority list.

A 3:30 group training goes smoothly. You finish, save your slides for reuse, and catch your breath for the first time all day.

From 4:00 to 5:00, you've blocked time to tame your inbox... but then your phone rings. It's the customer with the late PO, looking for an update. You assure them it's being handled and open a ticket with your delivery team while you're still on the call.

At 5:00, your day is technically over, but your inbox isn't.

Your manager texts: *"That PO situation all set?"*

You reply: "Ticket opened. Following up first thing tomorrow."

And at 6:03, you finally close your laptop. Not because everything's done but because you know how to prioritize what matters most.

This is the job. It's fast. It's unpredictable. It demands empathy, urgency, and strategic thinking — sometimes all in the same hour.

You won't always know what's coming. But when you build the right skills and show up ready, you'll become the calm in the chaos. The partner your customers trust. The person who figures it out.

Let's get to work.

Chapter 1

What is B2B Account Management?

I once sat in a 45-minute meeting with a procurement lead at a Fortune 500 company where the sole topic was industrial toilet paper.

That may sound like the setup to a bad joke, but it wasn't.

This single product impacted dozens of facilities, thousands of employees, and hundreds of thousands of dollars in annual spend. What seemed trivial on the surface turned out to be a surprisingly strategic conversation.

By the end of the call, we had mapped out a comprehensive transition plan, negotiated volume pricing, and uncovered a few additional product gaps that we could help fill. Within a year, the customer had doubled their annual spend with us and saved tens of thousands on supplies they already needed.

That's what account management looks like in the real world: business-critical conversations that don't always feel glamorous, but drive measurable value.

It's not about flashy sales tactics or elevator pitches. It's about showing up, staying curious, solving problems, and building partnerships that last.

And if you do it well, even a conversation about toilet paper can become a turning point in a long-term, high-value relationship.

Why This Book Exists

Behind-the-scenes work like that — solving real problems and creating real value — is what great account managers do every day. Yet for a role so essential, most people still learn it the hard way.

Although account management is a common role in almost every business that sells a product or service, few formal training programs exist to prepare individuals for the job. Most account managers learn by trial and error, picking up skills on the fly without a clear roadmap.

This book fills that gap.

It's not a textbook, and it doesn't aim to be. Instead, it's a practical guide written for today's sales professionals — whether you're brand new to the role or already years into your career — to help you level up faster, navigate challenges more confidently, and become the kind of account manager customers want to work with and companies fight to keep.

There's no rigid formula here, just real-world principles and actionable skills you can apply immediately. Paired with your own experience, they'll help you grow into a trusted advisor, strategic partner, and high-performing account manager.

The Focus: B2B Account Management

This book primarily focuses on business-to-business (B2B) account management, where I see the most opportunity and where I have spent my career.

B2B involves interactions between two businesses. In contrast, business-to-consumer (B2C) transactions happen when individuals buy directly from businesses (like you shopping online or in a store).

While some principles in this book apply to B2C account management, the tools, strategies, and examples are tailored to the B2B environment, where relationships are more complex and long-term.

Understanding the Difference: Account Management vs. One-Time Sales

Still wondering how an account manager differs from a traditional salesperson? Let's compare a few scenarios:

- When you buy furniture as a consumer, you may visit a store, talk to a salesperson, and make a one-time purchase. That salesperson helps you find what you need, completes the sale, and moves on to the next customer. Their goal is a quick transaction. Once the sale is done, the relationship typically ends.
- However, when a business needs furniture, the process becomes more complex. They work with a designated account manager, someone with whom they already have a relationship, or who is assigned to develop one. That account manager works to understand needs, then provides options, quotes, timelines, and brings in additional team members or specialists if needed.

The business purchase is more complex, and the account manager ensures it goes smoothly for the customer. The end result may be a single transaction, but more often, it's part of a growing, ongoing partnership.

This is just one small example of where B2B account managers exist, but it exemplifies how they differ from one-time salespeople.

Here's a simple illustration to help show the difference between an account manager and a one-time salesperson:

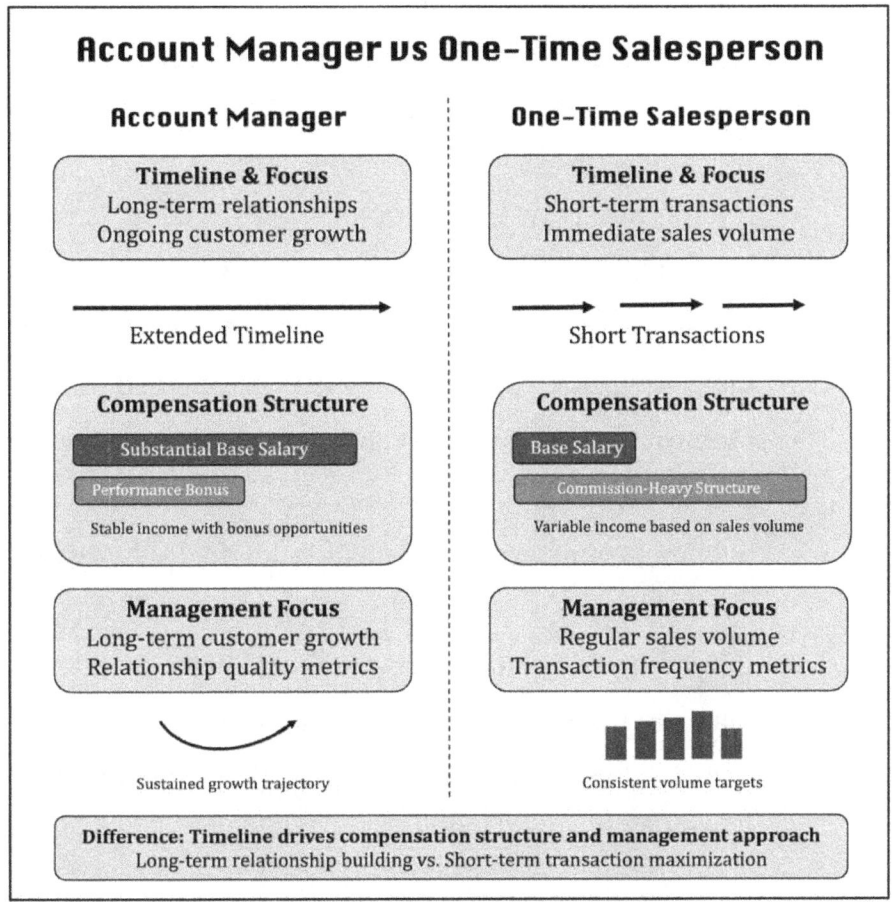

What Account Managers Actually Do

Account management is, at its core, a sales role, but not in the traditional, transactional sense. The key difference lies in the timeline and depth of the relationship. So what does that actually look like in practice? At a high level, account managers are responsible for:

- Building and maintaining relationships with key contacts at client companies.
- Acting as the main point of contact for customer questions, needs, and escalations.
- Identifying new sales opportunities within existing accounts (upsells, expansions, renewals).
- Collaborating internally with sales, operations, marketing, and support to deliver customer solutions.
- Monitoring account health, including revenue, engagement, and customer satisfaction metrics.
- Solving problems proactively, from delivery hiccups to product issues to process breakdowns.
- Communicating customer feedback back to internal teams to improve products, services, and processes.
- Driving long-term revenue growth while ensuring customer goals are achieved.

Timelines, Oversight, and Compensation

A one-time salesperson focuses on closing quick deals. Their compensation is typically commission-based, and their performance is measured by immediate sales volume. They usually work in sales offices or retail locations where customers come to them, and often have managers on-site providing significant oversight.

An account manager, on the other hand:

- Focuses on long-term revenue growth.
- Prioritizes relationships over transactions.
- Is typically paid a higher base salary with performance bonuses and possibly some commission.
- Works autonomously with minimal oversight, often outside of a traditional sales office.
- Goes where their customers are to meet with them.

Put simply, account managers aren't measured by how fast they can close a deal, but by how well they can grow, retain, and support a customer over time.

Why Relationships Matter

Account managers often spend weeks or months building a relationship before a sale occurs. They proactively identify customer contacts to work with by mining data from tools like Salesforce, ZoomInfo, and LinkedIn, or they inherit existing contacts. Either way, they generally must begin earning trust from the ground up.

Instead of relying on foot traffic or inbound leads, they create value by staying close to the customer, guiding, solving, and helping. They're the go-to contact for everything from minor purchases to major strategic deals. Relationships are key to successfully navigating this dynamic.

So, Why Do Companies Invest in Account Management?

If account managers don't drive immediate sales, why are they so valuable? Because they:

- Maintain and grow long-term relationships.
- Drive sustained revenue over time.
- Serve as the critical point of contact between two organizations.
- Translate C-suite vision into real-world action by working at the operational level.

Without account managers, CEOs and founders would have to personally handle even the smallest deals. Account managers enable peer-to-peer communication across roles and levels, scaling the relationship and aligning resources more efficiently.

Who Account Managers Work With

Remember the toilet paper meeting from the start of the chapter? On the surface, it seemed like a low-level sourcing decision. But for that procurement lead — and for the business — it was a meaningful, high-impact conversation. It saved real money, solved a real problem, and strengthened the partnership.

It's also the kind of discussion no CEO wants to sit through, even if their company is the one that sells the toilet paper. But they absolutely expect someone on their team to own it. And more often than not, that someone is the account manager.

Account managers handle these critical day-to-day conversations. They represent the company in countless practical discussions that are necessary to keep business moving. Whether it's:

- A procurement lead sourcing raw materials.
- A systems engineer managing technical contracts.
- A government official designing a new process.
- Or a bakery owner trying to get the supplies they need to operate their small business.

Each relies on account managers to represent product offerings, address concerns, and deliver solutions that keep operations running.

Communication at Every Level

Great account managers interact across all levels of a customer's organization, from frontline workers to C-suite executives. They tailor their communication accordingly, understanding that each level has unique needs and expectations.

The ability to adapt your message, whether you're talking to a store clerk or a senior vice president, is a key skill that separates great account managers from good ones. This ability to flex your communication style isn't just a nicety, it's how you translate customer goals into actionable solutions inside your own organization.

More Than a Sales Role

Account management isn't traditional sales, and it isn't customer service either. It sits at the intersection of sales, customer success, and consulting.

Unlike a one-time salesperson whose primary goal is closing deals, account managers focus on building long-term partnerships. And unlike customer service teams who typically respond to inbound issues, account managers proactively guide the relationship toward growth and mutual success.

A great account manager acts as both a strategist and an advisor. You're not just moving products, you're helping customers solve business problems. Sometimes that means connecting them to the right solution. Other times, it means bringing in the right internal experts or shaping a creative path forward that wasn't immediately obvious.

It's a consultative role, built on curiosity, problem-solving, and trust. Your customers rely on you not just to deliver what they've already bought, but to help them figure out what comes next.

This is what makes account management one of the most dynamic roles in business. You balance relationship-building with business growth. You flex between detail-oriented execution and big-picture thinking. And the better you get at navigating those two worlds — the operational and the strategic — the more valuable you become.

What's in a Title?

"Account manager" is only one of many names for this role. You might also be called:

- Account Executive
- Customer Success Manager
- Relationship Manager
- Business Development Specialist
- Adoption Manager
- Client Partner
- And more

Titles often include modifiers such as "Strategic," "Enterprise," "Key," "Principal," "Regional," "National," "Global," "Senior," "Junior," or "Associate," which signal the scope, focus, or seniority of the role.

Regardless of the label, if you manage ongoing relationships between companies, you're doing the job of an account manager.

Here's a visual that helps show the various titles account managers might use:

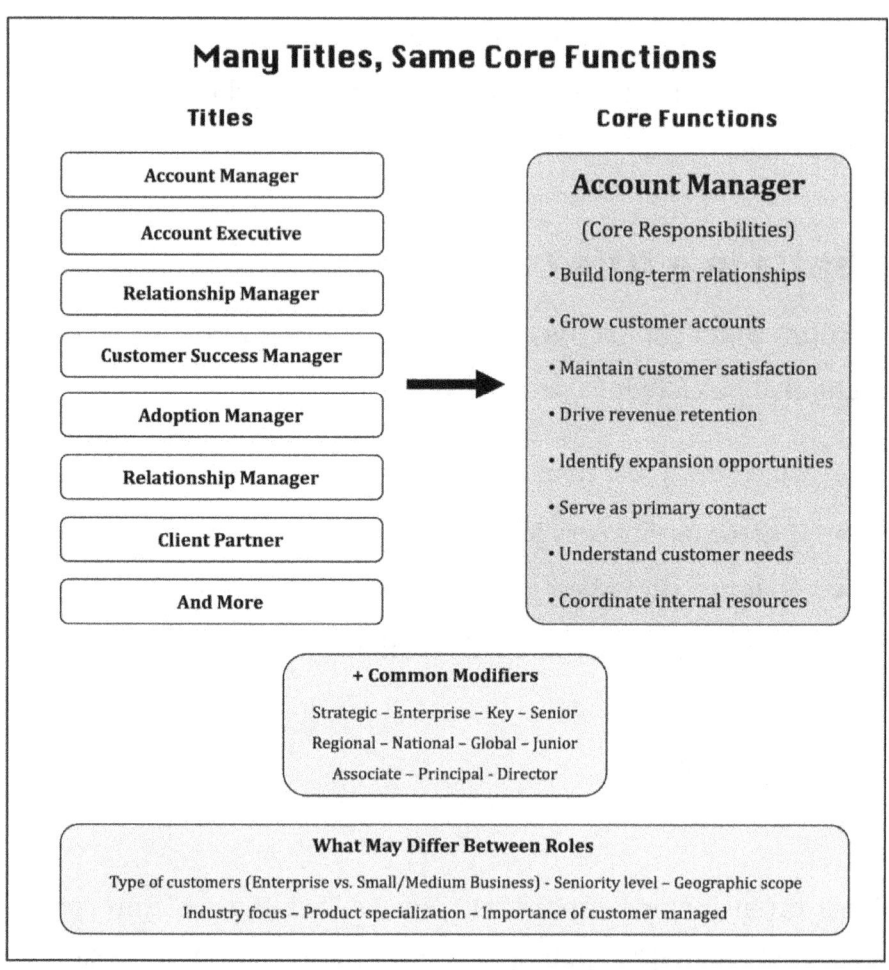

No One-Size-Fits-All Path

The role of an account manager varies widely by company and industry. Some people find success naturally; others work relentlessly to get there.

There's no single recipe, but there *is* a consistent set of skills that top account managers share. These skills are adaptable, learnable, and critical to your success, no matter where you start.

What You'll Learn in This Book

Throughout the rest of this book, we'll focus on the core skills that matter across every industry. I'll show you how to strengthen each one and apply it in practical, real-world situations.

You'll go through a series of "crash courses" that break each skill down into actionable steps or key elements. These crash courses are designed to take you from beginner to confident practitioner as efficiently as possible. I'll also use stories and real-world examples wherever possible to show how I've used each skill throughout my career in B2B account management.

Ready to Begin?

I once spent two hours preparing for a 15-minute call. I presented one slide, held one conversation... and it landed perfectly. That brief exchange led to a multi-year contract.

It worked because the presentation was precisely tailored to the customer's needs. And I knew what they needed because I had taken the time to build a relationship and listen carefully when they shared their goals.

Great account managers don't just react; they plan, they anticipate, and they show up ready to add value. It's not about having all the answers or saying the perfect thing in the moment. It's about knowing your customer well enough to offer the right solution at the right time.

That's account management in a nutshell.

It's not about doing more.

It's about doing the right things well.

No matter where you are in your account management journey, this book is your roadmap to success.

So, buckle up. You are stepping into one of the most challenging, rewarding, and growth-rich roles in the business world: B2B Account Manager.

Chapter 1 Review

Key Takeaways

- Account management is not about chasing one-time sales; it's about building long-term, value-driven partnerships.
- While the role may look different across organizations, the foundation is the same: consistency, trust, and follow-through.
- Great account managers know how to stay relevant, stay helpful, and stay engaged. No matter how the relationship evolves.

Reflection Questions

- How would you explain the value of account management to someone outside your industry?
- In your current role, are you focused more on closing short-term sales or driving long-term outcomes?

Apply It Now

- Write a one-paragraph definition of what account management means to you.
- Identify one relationship you could elevate from "vendor" to "partner." What's the first step toward making that shift?

Chapter 2

The Skills That Set You Apart

Every account management role is a little different, shaped by your company, your customers, and your industry. But the skills that drive success are universal, and if you master them, you'll thrive in any environment.

This chapter offers a high-level overview of each core skill. In the chapters ahead, we'll go deep into how to sharpen them, apply them, and use them to deliver exceptional outcomes for your customers and your career.

While we'll explore each skill in its own right, remember that they don't operate in isolation. Great account managers don't master one skill at a time; they weave them together in real-world situations. What follows is a practical snapshot of each skill: what it is, why it matters, and how it connects to the broader role.

Communication: Email and Verbal

Clear, effective communication is the foundation of every account manager's success. Whether you're in person, on a call, or writing an email, your job is to bridge two organizations, and that only works if information flows clearly, professionally, and consistently in both directions.

Communication happens in two primary forms: email and verbal. Both are essential, and mastering when and how to use each is a core part of the job. But it's not just about clarity, it's also about tone, professionalism, and timing. How you communicate often matters as much as what you communicate. We'll go deeper into those nuances later in this book.

Email is the backbone of most account management. It can be warm (to someone you already know) or cold (to someone new). Emails are how you follow up, align internally, recap meetings, confirm next steps, and keep projects moving. Writing clear, timely, and purposeful emails is a superpower in this role.

Verbal communication happens in meetings, phone calls, and video calls. In-person meetings are great for building rapport. Phone calls are perfect for quick clarifications or check-ins. Virtual meetings blend the two, offering flexibility without the need for travel.

Each format has its strengths and limitations. Your ability to shift between them and strike the right balance of clarity, tone, and professionalism is what separates average account managers from great ones.

The choice of whether to speak or write matters more than most people realize. If your message is emotionally sensitive, likely to create confusion, or requires quick back-and-forth, it's usually better handled live. If it's purely informational, needs a record, or requires careful wording, writing is often the better route. Great account managers learn to read the moment and choose the format that creates the most clarity and impact.

Great communication lays the groundwork, but it's not just about what you say, it's about what you hear. That's where listening and responding come in.

Listening and Responding

The best account managers listen for more than just answers. They pay attention to what's said, what's not said, and how it's said, catching tone, hesitation, and subtext that might reveal an unstated concern or hidden opportunity.

This also applies to written communication. Listening over email means reading between the lines. Are they feeling frustrated? Rushed? Unsure? Small cues often tell a bigger story.

But listening is only the first step. What you do with what you hear is where impact begins. Responding is where trust is built.

A great response shows that you've heard, understood, and are ready to help. Whether that means answering a question, clarifying a next step, or offering a thoughtful follow-up. The right response keeps conversations moving forward.

Just as importantly, listening is the foundation for handling objections. You can't overcome a concern you didn't hear, or didn't recognize beneath the surface. The stronger your listening, the easier it becomes to navigate objections with confidence and empathy.

With a stronger ear for what's beneath the surface, you're better equipped to turn obstacles into openings. Listening isn't passive; it's an active tool for finding problems to solve and value to add.

Once you're tuned in to what your customers are really saying, the next step is turning that understanding into trust. That's the essence of relationship building.

Relationship Building

One of the most defining skills in account management is the ability to build meaningful, long-term relationships, often from the ground up. Business relationships frequently start with cold introductions and limited context. Turning that into a multi-year, high-value relationship requires showing up reliably, adding value early, and proving you're someone worth partnering with over the long haul.

Even relationships that seem effortless by year five likely began with an awkward 30-minute intro meeting. **The ability to build trust and rapport quickly, even with limited information about the other person, is what sets account managers apart as relationship-driven professionals.**

Strong relationships are powerful, but true differentiation comes from going beyond expectations, and that's where customer obsession begins.

Customer Obsession

Great account managers go beyond meeting or exceeding expectations; they put themselves in their customer's shoes and genuinely obsess over their experience as a customer. Sometimes, they become so embedded in their customer's business that it can be hard to tell which company's payroll they are on. While that level of involvement isn't always necessary, it's crucial if the customer expects that depth of partnership.

Customer obsession means fully understanding your customer's needs and proactively finding solutions. This could involve advocating for new products or features, customizing a solution, or providing strategic recommendations. When you align your goals with your customer's and treat the relationship as a two-way street, long-term success follows.

Of course, obsessing over your customer's goals is only half the equation. You still have to communicate your ideas clearly and persuasively. That's where presentation building comes in.

Presentation Building

Being an account manager isn't all face time with the customer. A lot of the real work happens behind the scenes, especially when preparing for meetings. Building presentations is a core skill that involves gathering data, refining your message, and organizing visuals that support your pitch.

Sometimes you'll start with a pre-approved deck from your company. Other times, you'll build something from scratch. Either way, your ability to create a clear, compelling presentation is critical to moving deals forward, whether you're presenting to internal leadership or external customers.

But building a good presentation isn't just about putting data on slides; it's about visual storytelling. Knowing how to guide your audience through a narrative, highlight what matters, and avoid overwhelming them with information is critical to success. In the full chapter on presentation building, we'll go deeper into how to use structure, visuals, and clarity to make your message stick.

While a great presentation deck is a crucial tool, it's only as strong as the person delivering it. Now let's look at what it takes to bring your message to life in the room.

Presenting, Pitching, and Selling

Building the deck is one skill. Delivering it confidently and turning slides into sales is another.

Your presentation is where your ideas come to life, whether through PowerPoint, PDF, or anything else. But the visuals are only part of it; your delivery, confidence, and ability to connect with your audience matter just as much.

The goal of a presentation is to lead into a pitch where you'll offer something for your customer to consider or act on. This might be a product, a service, a software solution, or even a strategic partnership. An account manager's job is to frame whatever it is that you are pitching in a way that's relevant, valuable, and easy to say "yes" to. Even if the "yes" doesn't happen immediately.

Even the best pitch doesn't guarantee a "yes," and getting a "yes" doesn't mean the job is done. Whether you get a positive response or not, what happens next is just as important.

Follow-Up and Follow-Through

Follow-up happens when a pitch doesn't lead to an immediate answer. Great account managers stay engaged, provide new context, and keep the conversation moving. It's not about chasing a quick win, it's about supporting long-term relationships. A "no" today can easily turn into a "yes" tomorrow if you continue to show value and build trust.

But follow-up isn't only for stalled sales, it's also how account managers maintain momentum after delivery. Checking in, reinforcing value, and ensuring satisfaction are key parts of how account managers drive renewals, upsells, and long-term success.

On the flip side, follow-through begins after the customer says "yes." That's when the real work starts: coordinating fulfillment, aligning internal teams, and ensuring that what was promised gets delivered. **Unlike one-time sellers who disappear after the deal closes, account managers stay accountable.** They don't disappear, they deliver.

Following through with discipline builds trust. But doing it in the face of change and ambiguity? That takes flexibility and creativity.

Flexibility and Creativity

Flexibility helps you adapt to customer needs and changing industries. If you're only comfortable with one type of customer or solution, your growth will be limited. Being flexible enables you to transition smoothly between roles, customers, and sectors.

Creativity complements flexibility. Whether solving a complex customer problem or reimagining how to pitch a new offering, creativity helps you stand out. The ability to craft unique solutions by integrating ideas from multiple sources is a huge advantage in account management.

Together, flexibility and creativity make you a problem solver, and that's what customers value most.

Flexibility lets you adjust in the moment. But staying sharp over time requires something else: rapid learning and resourcefulness.

Rapid Learning and Resourcefulness

Top-performing account managers aren't just knowledgeable, they're relentlessly curious and surprisingly scrappy. In a role where customer questions shift fast and certainty is rare, your real value comes not from having every answer, but from how quickly you can track them down and how confidently you follow through.

You don't need to be the subject-matter expert in the room. But you do need to learn fast, think critically, and know how to tap into the right tools and teammates to get unstuck. Whether that means digging through internal documentation, asking smart questions across departments, or searching like a pro, your resourcefulness is what keeps momentum alive when clarity is lacking.

When you respond with speed, accuracy, and confidence, even after initially admitting you didn't know something, you build trust. Over time, your ability to learn and adapt becomes a key part of your professional brand. In account management, that brand can be the difference between being seen as a helpful vendor or a truly strategic partner, and it's something that customers notice.

Rapid learning and resourcefulness are how you stay valuable in a world that never stops moving.

Being quick to find answers is important, but understanding the bigger picture is what makes you truly effective. To manage accounts strategically, you also need to understand the numbers that tell the full story.

Understanding and Using Metrics

Last but not least, the ability to understand and use metrics is what enables you to manage accounts strategically. While data may not feel as exciting as communicating or pitching, it's what reveals where your accounts are thriving, where they're struggling, and where your time is best spent.

Too often, reporting is seen as a chore. But when approached with the right mindset, metrics become a strategic tool. Knowing your numbers allows you to tell your story, advocate for your customers, and prove your impact.

From engagement tracking to renewal forecasting and trend analysis, metrics help you work smarter, focus your efforts, and show the value you bring.

What's Next

Now that we've outlined the essential skills every account manager needs, we'll take a closer look at each one in the chapters ahead. You'll learn how to strengthen each skill and apply it with confidence, so you can build the foundation needed to become a truly exceptional account manager.

As we go deeper, remember: these skills are most powerful when used together. **The sooner you master them, the sooner you become the kind of partner customers fight to keep.**

Before we dive into the next chapter, let's take a step back and look at the whole picture. Here's a quick snapshot of the core skills every great account manager needs to master.

Critical Skills of an Account Manager

Universal skills that translate across all industries and companies

Communication Master email and verbal communication across all channels	**Listening & Responding** Build trust and open doors through active listening
Relationship Building Turn cold interactions into lasting partnerships	**Customer Obsession** Understand and advocate for your customer's needs
Presentation Building Prepare compelling materials from data driven sources	**Presenting, Pitching, & Selling** Your presentation is your pitch, and your pitch leads to your sale
Follow-Up & Follow-Through Persist after "no," deliver after "yes"	**Flexibility & Creativity** Adapt approaches and create unique solutions
Rapid Learning & Resourcefulness Learn fast and think critically	**Understanding & Using Metrics** Understand and advocate for your customer's needs

Chapter 2 Review

Key Takeaways

- There are core skills that, when mastered, can elevate you into a top-performing account manager.
- You don't need to be perfect at every skill, but you do need to use them together. Real success comes from how they work in combination.
- Consistency beats brilliance. Show up, follow through, and focus on steady improvement.

Reflection Questions

- Which of these skills are already your strengths? Which ones would benefit from additional focus?
- How do you respond when multiple skills are tested at once, such as during high-pressure meetings or complex negotiations?

Apply It Now

- Choose one skill to improve this quarter. Write down a simple weekly plan to strengthen it.
- Ask a trusted peer or mentor for honest feedback on one of your core skills after your next client or internal meeting.

Chapter 3

Email Communication

I once sent what I thought was a perfectly clear email to one of my most important customers. It was a status update on a pricing change, and I needed their approval to move forward. I recapped the context, outlined the options, and ended with: "Let me know if this works for you."

I didn't hear back.

A few days later, I followed up. Still no reply.

A week went by, and I finally got a message from the customer. It said: *"Sorry, I wasn't sure if you needed something from me."*

That was the moment it hit me. I hadn't actually asked for anything. I'd written a paragraph that danced around a decision, but never made the ask explicit. No wonder they didn't respond.

I rewrote the email, this time with one short line at the top: "Can you approve Option B by Friday so we can begin implementation?"

The reply came within an hour: *"Approved. Thanks for clarifying."*

That experience taught me something simple but powerful: vague writing leads to vague results. If you want action, your message needs purpose. And that starts with how you write.

Account managers are a proxy for the business, whether that's a CEO, founder, or brand. And how you show up in writing is often your first impression. It's how you deliver updates, confirm decisions, and keep momentum across busy calendars and global teams.

Your ability to write clear, concise, and well-timed emails has a direct impact on your success. Whether you're sharing a critical update, responding to a question, or nudging a stalled initiative forward, great email habits build trust and drive action. Customers and colleagues alike will judge your company by how you communicate, so make every message count. That starts with how you show up in writing.

What Is Effective Communication?

At its core, effective communication means conveying a message clearly, concisely, and with the intended meaning fully understood by the recipient. That last part is key: if your message is misinterpreted or not understood at all, it can create confusion, damage trust, or derail progress. Therefore, precision matters.

Why Email Still Reigns

Email remains a critical tool for one simple reason: it's asynchronous and scalable. You don't need your customer to be available in real-time to communicate. Emails can be sent, reviewed, and responded to on the recipient's timeline, making it a low-friction, high-efficiency medium.

Emails also serve as:

- A record of agreements and discussions.
- A formal channel for recapping meetings or confirming decisions.
- A reference point to document accountability and next steps.

The Four Types of Account Manager Emails

Email may seem like one simple tool, but not all emails serve the same purpose. As an account manager, your ability to adapt your tone, structure, and level of detail to the situation is critical. Broadly, email communication falls into four types based on two key distinctions:

- **Cold vs. Warm** - Does the recipient know you or expect your message?
- **Internal vs. External** - Are you communicating with someone inside your company or with a customer, partner, or prospect?

Cold Emails

A cold email is sent to someone who may not know you or is not expecting your message. These are usually outreach efforts designed to start a conversation or open the door to a meeting, not to close a deal.

Cold emails allow you to scale your outreach efforts and engage more potential customers than cold calls typically allow. The advantage? Recipients can respond on their own time rather than being caught off guard by a phone call.

> **Pro Tip: Focus On Opening Doors, Not Closing Deals**
>
> You're not a call center operator. Your goal is a long-term relationship, not a quick transaction. A cold email should start a dialogue, not try to close a deal.

Warm Emails

Warm emails are sent to contacts who already know you or are expecting to hear from you, or have been introduced by someone else. These emails allow for more targeted, detailed communication and carry an expectation of a response.

The value in a warm email isn't just in receiving a reply; it's what the response contains: an update, a decision, a request for more information, etc.

If the contact hasn't been introduced or isn't expecting your message, treat it like a cold email to avoid assuming familiarity.

Internal Emails

These are messages exchanged with colleagues within your company. They include updates to your manager, coordination with partner teams, answering questions, escalating issues, or requesting support.

Account managers often spend a significant portion of their time on internal communication via email due to the remote and autonomous nature of the role. Fewer in-office interactions mean more digital collaboration.

Internal emails are also a useful way to:

- Document tasks and decisions
- Create accountability
- Track requests and follow-ups

External Emails

These are the messages you send to clients, prospects, or external partners. They typically make up the majority of an account manager's email workload.

A single email from a customer can lead to:

- A dozen outbound emails
- Research and cross-functional coordination
- Escalations or scheduling follow-ups

Sometimes you'll respond. Other times, you'll initiate to recap meetings, clarify next steps, or request decisions. Regardless, email is where much of your relationship management and business development will happen.

The Big Picture

Mastering email isn't optional; it's one of the fastest ways account managers build trust, drive momentum, and show professionalism.

Whether you're writing warm intros, cold outreach, or internal updates, the ability to write a strong, effective email is a must-have skill. The good news? It's a learnable skill. Like any craft, it improves with practice, structure, and attention to detail.

Up next, we'll break down:

- How to structure effective emails
- Subject lines that get opened
- Tone and professionalism
- Follow-up techniques
- Common mistakes to avoid

With the right email approach, you'll position yourself to communicate with clarity, build credibility, and drive results — one message at a time.

> **Pro Tip: Great Emails Are Just the Start**
>
> A perfect email doesn't solve anything by itself. It moves the ball forward. Your follow-up, fulfillment, and responsiveness are what turn great writing into real-world results.

– A Crash Course in Writing Emails That Get Results –

Writing a Cold External Email

Cold emails are your door-openers. Here's how to write one that gets noticed and earns a reply.

Part 1 – The Subject Line

The subject line is the most important part of a cold email. It's the first thing a recipient sees and often determines whether your message is opened or deleted.

Rule #1: Keep it simple and avoid language that triggers spam filters. Common red flags include:

- Excessive use of all caps
- Alarmist phrases like "ALERT" or "Act now!"
- Sales-heavy jargon or misspelled words

Example: "ALERT Savings Imside!!!"

This kind of subject will likely land your email in the spam folder or be ignored altogether.

Instead, use something clean and professional. Often, just the name of your business works well. If the recipient won't recognize your company, include something informative but still vague enough to create curiosity. If you're reaching out based on an event, connection, or piece of news, reference that.

Examples:

- Following Up on Tuesday's Webinar
- Saw Your Post About Supply Chain Updates

> **Pro Tip: Subject Lines**
>
> Your subject line should catch attention without giving too much away. Your goal is to get them to open the email, not summarize the entire message upfront.

Part 2 – The Message

You've written a subject line that gets your email opened. Now what?

Keep the message brief.

Busy professionals don't have time to read long blocks of text, especially from someone they don't know. Most cold emails should be four to six short sentences, ideally under 150 words.

Start with a one- to two-sentence intro explaining who you are and why you're reaching out.

> **Example:** "I'm Bill from *The Book on That*. You recently attended one of my webinars. Did you get the information you needed?"

Then, follow with one or two additional brief paragraphs, each no more than one or two sentences. If your message can't fit within that space, you're trying to say too much too soon.

Pro Tip: Avoid Going Too Deep in Cold Emails

Save details for a follow-up email or phone call after the recipient shows interest.

Part 3 – The Hook

Your message should include a clear call to action, also known as your hook. This could be:

- A simple ask for a reply.
- A request to schedule a quick meeting.
- A prompt to download something or review a proposal.

Example: "If you'd like to learn more, just hit reply. I'd be happy to share more information."

The hook should appear naturally in your second or third paragraph, not tacked on as an afterthought.

Part 4 – The PS (Optional)

A well-written P.S. can catch the reader's eye, especially if they're skimming.

Use it sparingly and only on your first cold email. Skip it on follow-ups.

Example: "P.S. Did you know reading this book can help you become a better account manager?"

Part 5 – The Signature

Keep it professional and minimal. Include: your name, title, company, contact information, and a method for scheduling time with you (e.g., Calendly link).

Avoid clutter. Don't include: marketing slogans, upcoming events, inspirational quotes, or evergreen promotional offers.

These additions make your message look more like spam and distract from the real purpose: getting a response.

Cold External Email Example

Below is a sample cold email that puts these principles into practice. Note the tone, structure, and how the hook is positioned.

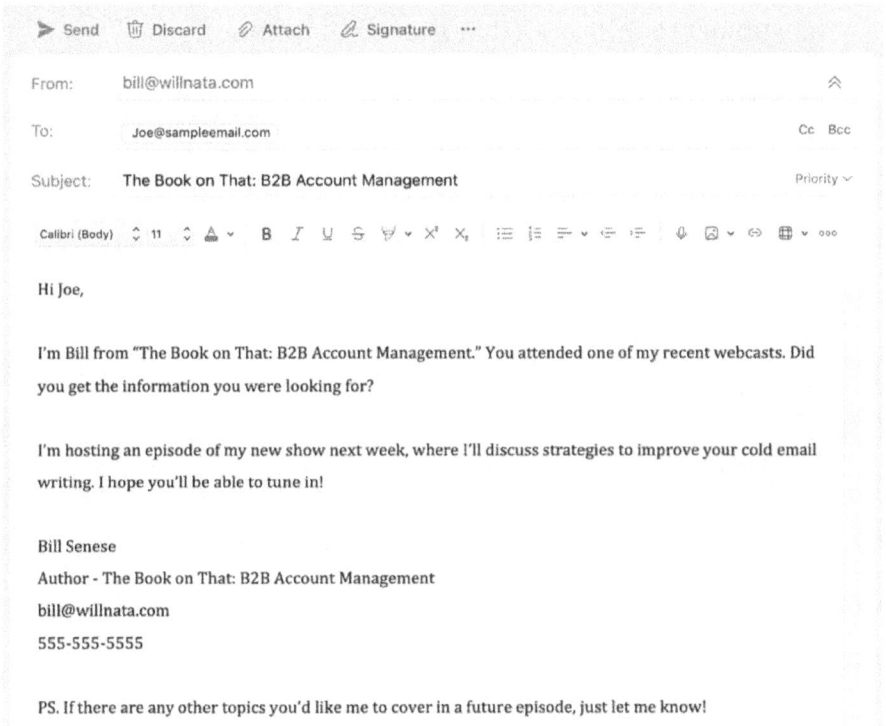

Writing cold emails can feel awkward at first, but they get easier. Focus on relevance, tone, and making it easy to reply.

Writing a Warm External Email

Warm emails are the day-to-day heartbeat of account management. They help you stay aligned, follow up with purpose, and move things forward without losing momentum.

Part 1 – The Subject Line

The subject line matters less in a warm email since your recipient already knows who you are. But it still serves a purpose: it helps the reader prioritize.

Use the subject to indicate what the email is about.

> **Examples:**
> - "Looking for Time to Connect"
> - "New Sprinkler Valve – Great Info"

Pro Tip: Spammy Subject Lines

Still avoid spammy language and misspellings. Even warm emails can be flagged by spam filters.

Part 2 – The Message

With warm emails, the message matters most. You can trust that the email will be read, so don't waste the recipient's time with fluff.

Avoid phrases like:
- "I hope this finds you well."
- "Just checking in..."

There's nothing wrong with checking in or inquiring about someone's state of being, but neither should be used as a first line in your email.

Instead, start strong with a one to two-sentence explanation of why you're reaching out. Use short paragraphs and bullets to make the message easy to skim. If your message is longer, structure it cleanly with:

- A clear opening
- Bullet points (if needed)
- Defined next steps

Example structure for a follow-up email:
1. Address outstanding questions.
2. Summarize updates.
3. Share next steps.
4. Request feedback or action.

Part 3 – The Hook

In warm emails, the hook is more specific and goal-oriented. If you're requesting data, setting a meeting, or needing a decision, make the ask clear.

Example:

- "Can I ask what you need this information for?"
- "Would you like to connect briefly to discuss further?"

Always give your message a purpose. Even in response emails, include a soft ask to keep the conversation moving.

Part 4 – The PS (Rarely Used)

Skip the PS. Put important content in the body of your email.

Part 5 – The Signature

Keep your signature professional. For warm emails:

- Include the basics: name, title, and contact information.
- In follow-up chains, simplify or drop the signature.
- Use a simple sign-off before your signature.

Pro Tip: Avoid Overly Formal Sign-Offs

Avoid stiff or outdated sign-offs unless they genuinely reflect your personality. Phrases like *"Sincerely,"* *"Professionally yours,"* or *"Respectfully"* can make your email feel too formal. In most cases, a simple *"Thanks,"* or even no sign-off at all, keeps the tone professional and better matches how people actually communicate today.

Warm External Email Examples

Now, let's walk through a few examples of warm emails in action. Note how each has a slightly different structure that supports the type of outreach and the goals it needs to accomplish.

Example 1: Warm Outreach

Below is an example of a warm outreach email. You'll see how it builds on an existing connection while staying clear, direct, and easy to respond to.

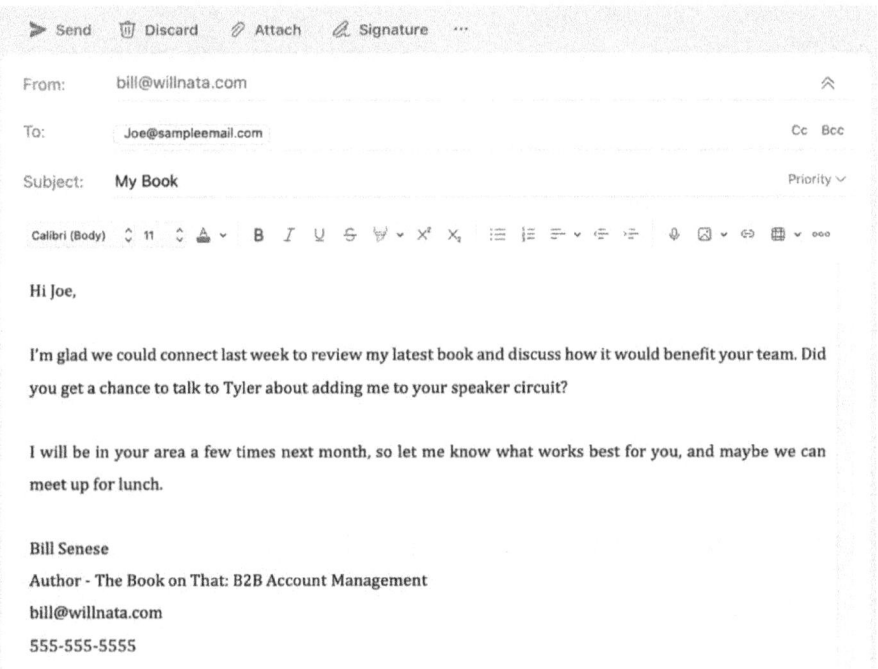

Example 2: First Response

Here's a sample reply to an initial message from a customer. Notice how it acknowledges the original email, provides a response to the ask that was received, and keeps the momentum going.

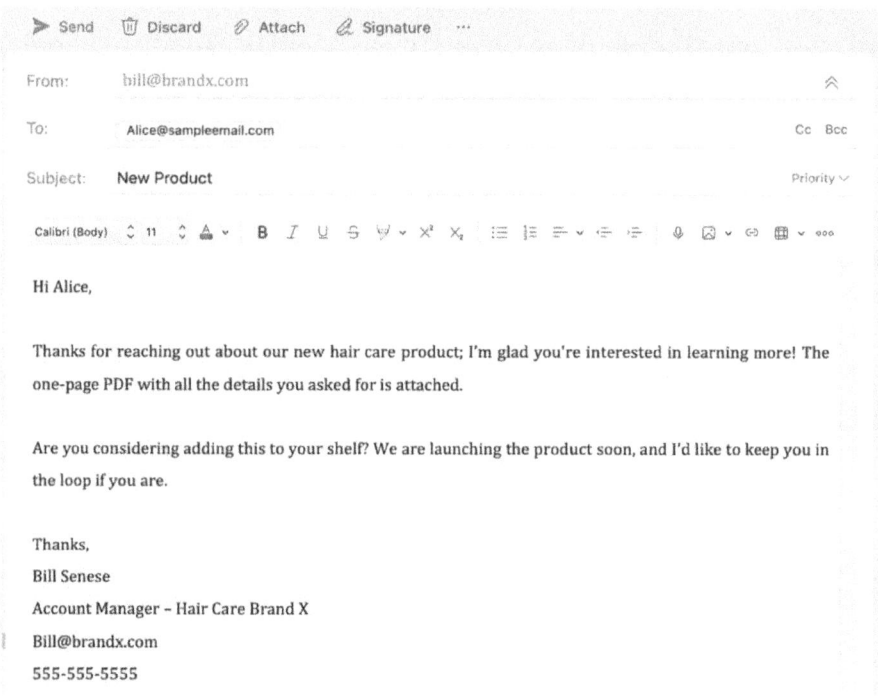

Example 3: Second, Third, etc. Response

This example shows what a second or third response might look like in an ongoing thread. The tone stays professional, the message is purposeful, and it avoids unnecessary repetition.

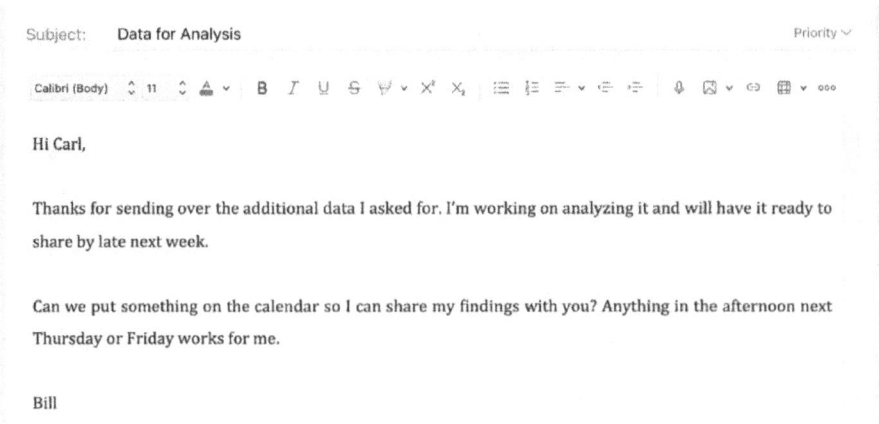

With warm emails, consistency and intent matter more than perfection. Keep practicing, and they'll become one of your most effective tools.

Writing an Internal Email

Internal emails are inherently warm because you're on the same team. But don't treat them casually. The same principles of clarity, brevity, and purpose apply.

Part 1 – The Subject

Your subject won't determine if the email is opened, but it will influence how quickly it's read.

- **Bad subject:** Really Need Your Help
- **Better subject:** Customer D Needs Document A

Give the recipient a preview of what's inside so they can prioritize it appropriately.

Part 2 - The Message

Internal emails can include more detail, especially when reporting results or explaining a process. However, always consider your recipient's time. To do this:

- Use bullets to break up dense content.
- Include only relevant details.
- If more information is needed, let them ask.

Less is more, especially when sending a message to leadership or cross-functional teams.

Part 3 - The Hook

Not every internal email needs a hook. Sometimes, you're just sharing info. But when making a request, be clear and specific:

- "Can you approve this by EOD Friday?"
- "Would your team be able to support this rollout?"

Even when no direct ask is involved, end with a clear close, like:

- "Let me know if this makes sense."
- "I'll proceed unless I hear otherwise."

Part 4 - The PS (Don't Use)

Rarely needed. Just say what you mean in the body of the message.

Part 5 – The Signature

Keep it simple. Your name, title, and maybe a phone number are all you need internally.

Internal Email Examples

Even when you're emailing people inside your own company, how you write matters. Here are a few examples of internal emails that are clear, respectful of time, and easy to act on.

Example 1: Basic Question/Request

This example illustrates a brief internal email requesting support. It's clear, direct, and makes it easy for the recipient to respond without needing to dig for context.

Subject: Book Shipment to Sanderson Books – Need Update

Hey Al,

My customer Sandersons is looking for an update on their order of our new title, 'The Book on That.' They'd like to know when it's going to be delivered.

Can you provide an updated delivery date so I can share it with the customer? Also, can you dig into what went wrong so we can make sure future shipments are delivered on time?

Thanks,
Bill

Example 2: Manager Update

Here's a sample update email to a manager. It highlights key points, avoids unnecessary detail, and shows how to communicate progress in a concise, professional way.

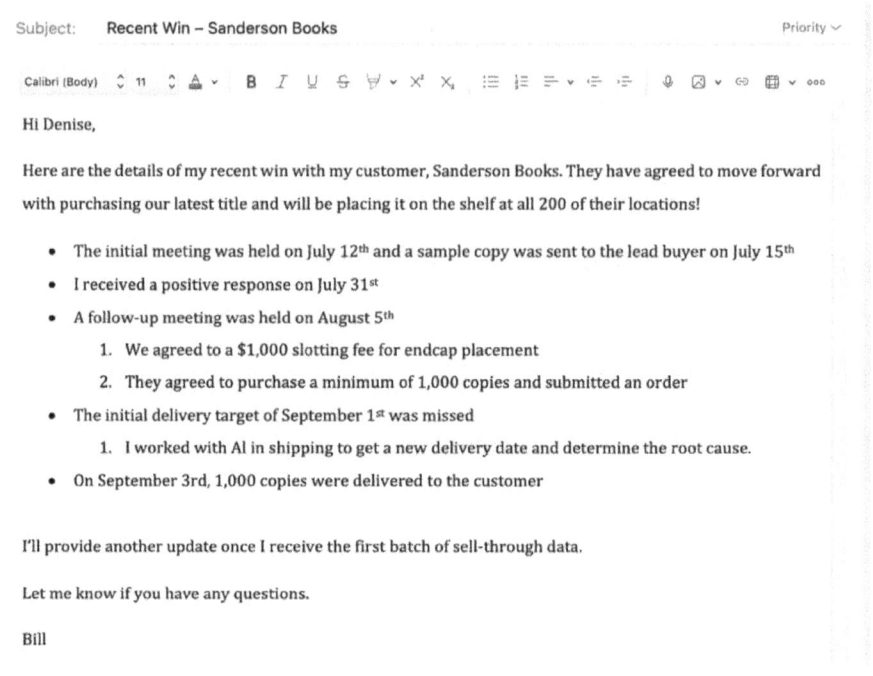

These examples aren't just templates; they're building blocks. With practice, you'll develop your own voice while still applying the same core principles.

Final Thought

If you've found a rhythm that works, keep using it. But if your emails aren't getting results, focus on the fundamentals: clarity, structure, and a strong hook. Every message is a chance to move something forward. Make it count.

Chapter 3 Review

Key Takeaways

- Email is one of the most frequently used tools in account management. But it is often one of the most overlooked when it comes to polish and strategy.
- A good email is clear, concise, and easy to skim. A great email drives results.
- Cold and warm outreach require different tones and structures; adapt accordingly.

Reflection Questions

- Do your emails make it easy for the recipient to reply or take action?
- When was the last time you re-read an email through the recipient's eyes before hitting "send"?

Apply It Now

- Select a recent email thread and revise one message to incorporate a more intentional and strategic structure.
- Practice writing one cold and one warm outreach email from scratch. Focus on a clear subject line, a sharp opening, a purposeful hook, and a professional tone.

Chapter 4

Verbal Communication

A few years ago, I was working with a mid-sized customer who had recently expanded into a new market. We'd been emailing back and forth for weeks, trying to finalize a rollout plan. Everything seemed to be moving forward until suddenly, they went quiet.

No replies. No approvals. Nothing.

I reread the last few emails and realized I might've overloaded them with too much detail and not enough clarity. So instead of sending another message, I picked up the phone.

"Hey," I said, "I know your inbox is a war zone. Thought I'd try this the old-fashioned way."

The customer actually laughed. *"Thank you,"* they said. *"Honestly, I've been meaning to reply, but I had no idea what you were asking for in that last email."*

We spent ten minutes on the phone. I clarified a few points, adjusted the plan, and by the end of the call, we had a verbal agreement.

That call salvaged momentum. But more importantly, it reminded me: some things can't be fixed over email. Sometimes, you need to hear each other's voices to get back on track.

You can't build trusted partnerships through emails and attachments alone. At some point, you have to speak. That's where verbal communication becomes your most powerful tool.

Verbal communication takes many forms, each with its own strengths for delivering a message, building relationships, and driving momentum. While email may be the most commonly used communication channel for account managers, verbal communication is a close second — and it often proves more powerful. Whether you're meeting in person, hosting a video call, or making a phone call, speaking directly with customers helps cut through the noise, convey tone, and deepen the connection.

Unlike email, verbal interactions are immediate. They allow you to read and respond to emotional cues in real-time. You can clarify misunderstandings, express empathy, and adjust your delivery based on the customer's response — none of which are easily accomplished through written text.

Verbal communication should often be the default when:

- There's ambiguity.
- Emotions are running high.
- A deal is stuck.
- Multiple stakeholders need alignment quickly.

Why Verbal Communication Matters

Verbal conversations allow for genuine human connection. They break down the barriers that can exist in written communication and help account managers build trust through tone, timing, and presence. While email is often used to confirm details or formalize agreements, verbal exchanges are where relationships are built and objections are handled.

> **Pro Tip: Speak Instead of Writing When...**
> - The message involves emotion, ambiguity, or nuance.
> - You need fast back-and-forth or live feedback.
> - Misunderstanding could damage trust or slow progress.

Types of Verbal Communication

Account managers typically rely on three core types of verbal communication:

1. **In-Person Meetings**
2. **Virtual Meetings**
3. **Phone Calls**

Each format has its strengths. Here's a quick snapshot of when to use which, and where to go next in the book to sharpen that skill.

Three Formats, Three Use Cases

Communication Type	Best For	Explored In
In-Person	Building trust, resolving issues	Chapter 5
Virtual	Efficiency with face-to-face presence	Chapter 8
Phone Calls	Speed, quick updates, real-time clarity	Chapter 4

In-Person Meetings

Some account managers rarely meet customers face-to-face. Others meet in person regularly. The industry, geography, or the nature of your accounts will dictate just how often you meet your customers in person. Regardless of your role, in-person communication remains one of the most powerful tools for deepening customer relationships.

Examples of in-person engagements:
- One-to-one meetings
- Small group meetings
- One-to-many meetings

The goal of an in-person meeting is to create a connection, build rapport, and solve complex problems collaboratively.

We'll take a deep dive into in-person meetings in later chapters, examining various engagement types in more detail.

Where Each Meeting Type Is Covered	
Meeting Type	**Explored In**
One-to-One and Small Group	Chapter 6
One-to-Many	Chapter 7

Virtual Meetings

Video conferencing tools like Zoom, Teams, and Google Meet make virtual meetings almost as effective as in-person ones, when used well.

Benefits:

- Face-to-face connection without travel.
- Real-time conversation for faster alignment.
- Ability to share screens, review materials, or demonstrate solutions.

When possible, turn cameras on. Face-to-face communication, even virtual, strengthens trust and reduces misunderstandings. However, virtual meetings depend on strong internet connections, the willingness of both parties to use video, and the ability to focus and stay engaged (i.e., avoid multitasking).

Off the Record vs On the Record

One important nuance of verbal communication is whether it's on or off the record, and how that affects what people share. Verbal conversations are typically off the record, which often leads to more candid, honest discussions. That said, some virtual conversations may be recorded for training or documentation. When recording, keep these points in mind:

- Always notify participants and obtain consent.
- Consider whether recording may hinder openness in the conversation.

If candid feedback or emotional insight is essential, avoid recording unless absolutely necessary.

Phone Calls

Phone calls are the fastest, most accessible form of verbal communication. They're ideal for quick check-ins, answering time-sensitive questions, or maintaining momentum between meetings.

Not all phone calls are created equal. There are two types, and how you use them makes all the difference.

- **Scheduled calls:** These should be treated like virtual meetings, with a clear agenda, a designated time block, and intentional follow-up.
- **Unscheduled calls**: These should be used sparingly. Most professionals' calendars are packed, and unexpected calls often interrupt focus or go unanswered.

> **Pro Tip: Unscheduled Phone Calls**
>
> When making or receiving an unscheduled call:
>
> - Be concise and respect the other person's time.
> - Lead with "Is this a good time?" or "Do you have a few minutes?"
> - Respect signals like hesitation or background noise.

While phone calls are often used to build on existing relationships, you may wonder where cold calling fits in.

What About Cold Calling?

Although cold calling has its place in sales, it's not the best use of time for most account managers, especially those managing a mature book of business. Today, cold emailing to schedule a call is usually a more effective — and more respectful — way to engage a new contact.

> **Note:**
>
> This book will not focus on cold-calling strategy, as account management is more relationship-driven than transactional, and cold-calling is not an area I believe B2B account managers should spend a significant amount of their time.

Mastering Verbal Communication

Like any skill, verbal communication can be learned, practiced, and refined. **Even if you're not naturally confident speaking with customers, you can master the art of conversation over time.**

In the next four chapters, we'll break down how to lead verbal interactions across every key format: from in-person meetings and small-group discussions to one-to-many presentations and virtual calls.

Final Thought

Whether you're walking into a boardroom or logging onto Zoom, your ability to lead the conversation is what sets top account managers apart. First up: how to make the most of your in-person time, whether it's a one-to-one meeting or a room full of decision-makers.

Chapter 4 Recap

Key Takeaways

- Verbal communication builds connection, trust, and clarity in ways that email cannot.
- Use it when stakes are high, emotions are involved, or nuance matters.
- Prioritize scheduled conversations for complex topics and use unscheduled calls only when absolutely necessary.

Reflection Questions

- Are you using verbal communications strategically, or only when problems arise?
- What does your tone and delivery say about your confidence, clarity, and preparation?

Apply It Now

- Identify one situation this week where speaking would have a greater impact than sending an email, and then have or schedule the conversation.
- Before your next conversation, write down your key message in one sentence. Then deliver it with intention.

Chapter 5

In-Person Meetings

I once flew across the country for a 30-minute meeting. No slides, no formal agenda; just a conversation that needed to happen face-to-face. Tensions had been building over weeks of back-and-forth emails. The customer was frustrated, and momentum had stalled. But once we were sitting across the table, things shifted. Misunderstandings cleared up. Tones softened. By the end of the meeting, we weren't just aligned, we were brainstorming new ideas together.

That meeting turned into one of the most valuable partnerships of my career. And it never would've happened on Zoom.

That's the power of showing up in person. It's become rare, but it remains incredibly effective. In today's virtual-first world, that kind of presence is unexpected, and it stands out.

Not long ago, face-to-face meetings were the standard in managing B2B relationships. Whether checking in, solving problems, or pitching solutions, you did it across the table, not over a computer screen. You built relationships at the customer's office, over coffee, or wherever you could schedule a visit.

But times have changed. The rise of remote work, tighter travel budgets, and the widespread adoption of virtual meeting tools have led to most interactions shifting online. While this shift offers efficiency, it also creates a competitive advantage for those willing to show up in person.

Because they're no longer the norm, in-person meetings carry more weight. They require more effort, but they signal commitment and show customers you're willing to show up.

When done right, one well-prepared face-to-face meeting can do the work of ten virtual calls. This chapter will help you make every in-person meeting count by covering:

- Why in-person meetings still matter.
- The formats they typically take.
- The core skills that will help you stand out in the room.

Why In-Person Meetings Create an Edge

Some account managers avoid in-person meetings due to travel costs, time constraints, or personal preference. But those who embrace them gain access to broader industries, deepen client relationships, and create lasting impressions.

In-person meetings cut through the noise of packed inboxes and back-to-back video calls. They allow you to communicate with full presence. With your tone, body language, and focus all able to reinforce the value you bring.

You also pick up on subtle dynamics: office culture, hallway chatter, and reactions that wouldn't come across over a webcam. You become more than a voice or a screen; you become *real*.

Common In-Person Meeting Formats

Understanding the structure and expectations of each format will help you adjust your approach and maximize impact.

1. One-to-One Meetings

These are the foundation of relationship-building. Typically, you'll meet with your main point of contact, solo or with a teammate shadowing. One-to-one meetings are your best chance to:

- Share updates.
- Pitch new solutions.
- Solve problems together.
- Brainstorm ideas.
- Strengthen trust.

2. Small Group Meetings

These involve 2–5 people from the customer's side and may include additional stakeholders from your own team. Small group meetings are ideal for:

- Business reviews
- Strategic planning
- Decision-making conversations

If you've laid strong groundwork in one-on-one meetings, this is where your work becomes visible to a broader audience.

3. One-to-Many Meetings

In this format, you're presenting to a larger audience, often in a demo, training, or event-style setting. Examples of one-to-many meetings include:

- Product trainings
- Trade shows
- Vendor fairs
- Round-robin sessions

These sessions are less conversational and more presentation-driven. They test your ability to command attention, manage a room, and deliver a clear and compelling message to multiple stakeholders simultaneously.

Being confident across all three formats allows you to work with different departments, navigate diverse personalities, and make an impact in any room.

– A Crash Course in In-Person Meetings –

Now let's explore what makes in-person meetings successful, and how to avoid the common traps that derail them.

Key 1 – Treat It Like the Opportunity It Is

In-person meetings are no longer routine; they're a statement. They say: "This matters." When someone makes room for you physically, they're offering time, space, and attention. Respect that effort by showing up ready to deliver.

Use the opportunity to:

- Strengthen trust.
- Reset a relationship.
- Uncover deeper insights.
- Move stalled deals forward.

Key 2 – Leverage What Virtual Can't Replicate

Face-to-face interactions provide advantages no screen can match:

- Faster trust-building through eye contact, tone, and body language.
- Real-time pivots when you see interest, confusion, or hesitation.
- Spontaneous insights from lobby chats or walking through the office.
- Unexpected visibility, like bumping into other stakeholders or executives.
- Deeper, more memorable connections.

You're not just observing. You're absorbing. Culture, tone, and priorities all surface when you're in the room.

Key 3 – Avoid the Pitfalls That Undermine Your Presence

Being there isn't enough. How you show up determines what people remember.

Avoid these mistakes:
- **Being late:** There's no grace period like in virtual meetings. Show up early.

- **Being unprepared:** You can't hide behind a screen. Know your material, anticipate questions, and have a plan.
- **Being rigid:** You can't just "put a pin in it" and move on. You need to be flexible, respond in real-time, and follow the conversation wherever it leads.
- **Being distracted:** Checking your watch or phone signals disinterest, even if unintentional.

I once made the mistake of checking my smartwatch multiple times during a meeting. I had received numerous messages, with each one buzzing my wrist, which caught my attention. My customer thought I was checking the time, signaling that our meeting wasn't important to me. Thankfully, they understood once I explained, but that won't always be the case. Put your devices in "Do Not Disturb" mode, including smartwatches, and give the customer your full attention.

Key 4 – Know When Face-to-Face is the Right Move

Not every touchpoint requires travel, but certain moments benefit from physical presence. Meet in person when:

- You're establishing a new relationship.
- You're leading a business review or strategic planning session.
- You're handling a sensitive topic or an escalating issue.

Additionally, events like trade shows, vendor fairs, and golf tournaments *are* "be there or miss out" opportunities, and you don't want to miss out.

Before we get into the core skills for in-person meetings, here's a quick reference to make sure you're showing up at your best:

In-Person Meeting Checklist

Quick-reference checklist: Make sure you've done the essentials before walking into the room.

- ✓ Set clear objectives
- ✓ Confirm the agenda
- ✓ Research the customer
- ✓ Dress intentionally and appropriately
- ✓ Arrive early, calm, and ready
- ✓ Bring printed materials or leave behinds
- ✓ Prepare key talking points
- ✓ Silence distractions

Core Skills for In-Person Meetings

Showing up sends a message. But how you show up is what leaves a mark. In-person presence carries weight. It signals commitment, builds trust, and creates lasting impressions. But to truly stand out, you need to show up with intention.

Think of the room as a stage and yourself as the face of your company. These six skills make sure you're ready when the spotlight hits.

Skill 1 - Appearance

You don't need a suit to make an impression, but you should look like you meant to show up the way you did. Authenticity matters, but so does intention. Show up looking prepared, polished, and confident, and match the tone of your audience.

- Sometimes "dressing the part" is worth it, especially when meeting executives in a more formal environment.
- If your outfit helps the conversation go more smoothly, it's a small investment for a better outcome.
- When in doubt, level up. It's easier to dress down than to dress up on the spot.

Be yourself, just make sure your "self" looks like they meant to be there.

Skill 2 – Punctuality

Be early. Always. Arrive early enough to:

- Clear security or check in at reception.
- Gather your thoughts and review your notes.
- Settle in so you're calm, composed, and ready to go.

Punctuality signals professionalism. Rushing in breathless at the last minute sets the wrong tone before you even say a word.

Skill 3 – Preparedness

In-person meetings require depth, not just presence.

Come ready with:
- A clear agenda and objectives for the meeting.
- Printouts, talking points, and visual aids.
- A defined purpose and next steps.
- Answers to, or at least informed perspectives, on likely questions.
- Research stakeholder roles, backgrounds, and recent company news to personalize the conversation.

Preparation boosts your confidence. Confidence builds trust. Trust drives business.

Skill 4 – Speaking and Presenting

When you speak, you lead the room. And in person, there's no mute button or second screen to hide behind. You need to communicate with clarity, display confidence, and control your tone, pace, and body language.

Visuals can help, but they should guide your message, not carry it.

We'll go deeper into presentation skills in Chapters 12 and 13, but for now, focus on this: **If you can't explain it well, you can't sell it well.**

Skill 5 – Personality

Your personality is your secret weapon. Don't water it down.

Be warm. Be real. Share small personal stories that build a connection. Let your customer see you as a person, not just a rep.

For example, I once brought up my family's lake house in Indiana during a conversation with a customer in California. It turned out his spouse had family in the area, and he'd been to the lake I went to every weekend as a child. That small connection point helped me build a relationship and became a recurring topic that we talked about in every future meeting.

Be yourself. But steer clear of divisive or overly personal topics until trust has been established. Relatability wins relationships.

Skill 6 – Quick Thinking and Good Memory

You won't have time to Google an answer in the middle of an in-person meeting. Instead, you'll need to:

- Think on your feet.
- Answer what you can confidently.
- Acknowledge what you don't know and promise to follow up.
    - **And when you say you'll follow up, do it.**

Taking notes is fine. Remembering what matters is better. Customers value responsiveness and follow-through more than getting every answer right in the moment.

Putting it All Together

In-person meetings require more planning, effort, and energy — but they're worth it. They help you cut through the noise, create genuine connections, and establish yourself as a trusted partner.

Final Thought

In a sea of virtual sameness, face-to-face stands out. It's the scenic route: slower, requiring more effort, but richer in impact and opportunity.

Anyone can show up on Zoom. The people who walk in the door are the ones who make a lasting impression.

Chapter 5 Recap

Key Takeaways

- In-person meetings accelerate relationship-building and foster deeper, more personal connections.
- Preparation is essential when meeting face-to-face. It reflects your professionalism and shows respect.
- Whether you have a one-on-one meeting or will be presenting in front of a full room, your presence makes a statement. Use the opportunity to make an impact.

Reflection Questions

- How do you shift your mindset and preparation when you will be meeting someone in person?
- What signals are you sending, verbally and non-verbally, when you show up in person?

Apply It Now

- Identify one customer who could benefit from an in-person meeting. Reach out and schedule a meeting.
- Before that meeting, and before every major face-to-face meeting, review the in-person meeting checklist shared earlier in this chapter.

Chapter 6

One-to-One and Small Group Meetings

A customer once invited me to their office for a simple one-on-one meeting. No agenda, no urgency; just a casual catch-up. I nearly declined, thinking I was too busy to make the trip and we could handle it over email. But I went.

What started as a simple check-in turned into a full-on strategy session. As we talked, he pulled in two colleagues from around the office. *"You should hear this,"* he told them. Within fifteen minutes, we were mapping out a solution on the whiteboard. By the end of the meeting, we had alignment from multiple departments and a path forward on a project that had been stalled for months.

If I hadn't shown up in person and made the most of an unexpected opportunity, that momentum never would've happened.

One-to-one and small group meetings are the heart of in-person customer interaction. They're where relationships are built, trust is earned, and deals take shape. Whether you're meeting one-on-one or with a handful of decision-makers, these formats offer a rare chance to listen closely, speak directly, and influence meaningfully.

Both formats demand presence, preparation, and the ability to read the room. But they play out differently. One-to-one conversations allow for depth. Small group meetings create opportunities for alignment and acceleration.

This chapter will show you how to handle both meeting types with confidence so you're ready, whether it's just you and one customer or a table full of decision-makers.

– A Crash Course in One-to-One Meetings –

First, let's explore how to make one-to-one meetings successful by showing up prepared, staying present, and turning conversation into momentum.

Part 1 – Before the Meeting

The best meetings begin long before you walk into the room.

Start with clear objectives, supported by a shared agenda that aligns expectations and sets the tone for a purposeful conversation. The agenda should answer questions like: What's the goal of the meeting? What topics need to be covered? What decisions, if any, do you hope to make?

Next, get the logistics right. In most cases, it's your job to go to them, not the other way around. That could mean a short drive, a flight, or even a multi-day trip. Confirm the location, the time, and the exact spot where you'll meet. Will you meet in the lobby, a specific room number, a restaurant, or somewhere more unique, like a golf course or arena?

If you're meeting off-site, such as at a restaurant, coffee shop, or sporting event, be mindful of the setting. Informal venues can lead to more open dialogue and allow for better relationship building. In some industries, customer entertainment is encouraged. In others, it's strictly off-limits. Know your audience, your company's policies, and the norms of your industry.

Finally, plan your travel with buffer time. Aim to arrive 10–15 minutes early, especially if it's an unfamiliar location. If there's a delay due to traffic, parking, or security check-in, you'll have time. If there's no delay, great, you'll be early, and that never hurts.

Part 2 – Arrival and Set Up

Once you've arrived at the meeting location, your job is to stay sharp and make a strong first impression before the meeting even begins.

At your customer's office, check in confidently and be prepared with your contact's first and last name. If you need to sign in, take a look at the sign-in sheet. Small details, like a competitor's recent visit, can offer helpful context.

Waiting in the lobby? Use the time to gather your thoughts, review your agenda, or prep your materials. These minutes can help you transition from travel mode to meeting mindset.

For off-site meetings, arrive early and get set up in advance. That might mean testing your laptop at the table or reviewing your notes quietly in the car. Either way, be fully ready before your customer walks in.

Be alert, be prepared, and look like you've done this before, even if it's your first time.

Part 3 – Introductions and Small Talk

Always greet your contact with a warm, professional welcome. If it's your first time meeting them, stand up, introduce yourself, and offer a handshake. If you've met before, use those first few minutes to catch up and break the ice.

Engage in light, positive small talk. Talk about your travel, the weather, recent news (non-controversial), or shared interests. Avoid discussing politics, religion, or any other topics that may be polarizing. And don't let this drag on. Five minutes or less is a good guideline. The exception? First-time meetings, where rapport-building is part of the purpose.

Part 4 – Running the Meeting

Once you're seated with your customer, whether across a conference table, at a restaurant, or side-by-side at a ball game, it's time to get to work.

Start by anchoring to the agenda or plan you prepared. That doesn't mean jumping into a script. It means setting a tone of clarity and intention: Here's what we're here to talk about, and here's what we're hoping to achieve. A quick reminder of the meeting's purpose shows you respect their time and frames the conversation effectively.

From there, stay focused on the objective. Your deck, if you're using one, should already be polished and practiced (see Chapter 12). That said, many one-to-one meetings aren't about presenting slides at all, they're often strategic conversations. Whether you're sharing updates, seeking alignment, or asking for a decision, the most important thing is to keep it a dialogue, not a monologue.

Ask good questions. Let your customer speak. Listen actively.

Avoid "show up and throw up" syndrome, where you talk for twenty minutes straight and forget to pause. Pull your customer into the conversation by asking questions like:

- "How does this line up with what you're seeing on your end?"
- "Is this still a top priority?"
- "Are we missing anything?"

Meetings are also your chance to pick up on subtle signals — such as hesitation, tone shifts, or side comments — that hint at deeper issues or hidden opportunities. Stay alert. And don't be afraid to pause and recalibrate. If the conversation veers off track but toward something meaningful, lean in.

As for tools, use your laptop only when necessary. If you're presenting, launch the deck and then close all unrelated apps. Turn off notifications. Better yet, disable Wi-Fi unless it's needed. Visual clutter and pop-ups can break focus and signal a lack of professionalism.

Not presenting? Close the laptop. Jotting notes by hand shows you're engaged and helps you avoid distractions. Customers may use their laptops freely, but you're there to be fully engaged. If you are taking notes, also jot down any internal observations. Things like potential concerns, organizational dynamics, or follow-up opportunities, not just what's said out loud.

Finally, keep an eye on the clock. Be mindful of how much time remains and adjust accordingly. If the meeting is running short, focus on the must-haves. If you're ahead of schedule, use the extra time to deepen the conversation, clarify next steps, or build rapport.

The meeting is your moment to deliver value. Whether you're answering questions, driving a decision, or simply listening well, make sure your customer leaves feeling heard, helped, and one step closer to their goals.

Part 5 – Wrapping Up

When the meeting nears its end, summarize what you've covered. Clarify any decisions that have been made, questions that remain unanswered, or follow-ups that are required. If time allows, deepen your relationship or ask for a quick office or facility tour, if appropriate.

If you're at a restaurant, plan to pick up the check. If your customer declines, accept it graciously and don't insist. At events like golf outings or games, there won't be a formal closing moment, so take opportunities throughout the event to guide the conversation and build rapport.

End with appreciation. A simple *"Thanks for making time today, this was valuable,"* goes a long way. Then, follow up with a recap email and any action items discussed.

The close of a meeting isn't just a wind-down; it's your last impression. Aim to leave your customer feeling heard, clear on next steps, and better off than they were an hour ago.

While one-to-one meetings are built for depth, small group meetings require a wider lens. One that captures multiple perspectives, dynamics, and decision-makers.

– A Crash Course in Small Group Meetings –

Small group meetings follow the same structure and etiquette as one-to-one meetings, but with a few key distinctions. Here's how to navigate the differences.

Shift 1 – Make Time for Introductions

With more people in the room, introductions matter. They establish roles and help everyone feel included.

Lead by introducing yourself and anyone joining from your side. Then, ask your primary contact to introduce their team. Plan for at least five minutes for this. If you don't, you'll risk rushing through the actual content.

Shift 2 – Spreading Your Attention

In group meetings, your attention becomes a resource, one that must be managed strategically.

Your primary contact should still receive the majority of your focus. They're likely your main decision-maker or day-to-day point of contact, and the person you'll be following up with most directly. But that doesn't mean others in the room should be ignored, far from it. Everyone present should feel acknowledged and engaged, especially if they've taken time to join.

Here's how to balance the room effectively:

- Make eye contact with everyone, not just your primary contact.
- Acknowledge and build on comments from other attendees.
- Direct questions broadly ("How do you all think this would work for your team?") to encourage group participation.
- Observe body language. If someone looks confused, skeptical, or eager to chime in, invite them in with a quick, "Looks like you might have a thought, anything you'd add here?"

If someone is clearly shadowing or observing, like a junior team member or intern, they don't need equal airtime, but they still deserve inclusion. Greet them when the meeting begins. Make occasional eye contact. Involve them without shifting the conversation off-course. These small gestures help them feel respected, and your primary contact will notice your professionalism.

On the other hand, if your contact brings a peer, senior leader, or cross-functional partner, your dynamic should shift. In these situations, you're often managing internal politics as much as content delivery.

Treat each stakeholder as an active participant, even if they're quiet. Don't assume influence based on title alone, but do recognize that everyone plays a role in shaping the outcome.

Think of group meetings as multi-audience presentations. You're not giving each attendee an equal share of the spotlight, but you are making sure no one feels left in the dark. These meetings are your best opportunity to start multi-threading, building trusted relationships beyond just your primary contact. Just make sure you loop in your main contact and give them credit along the way.

By the time the meeting ends, you want every person at the table to feel seen, heard, and respected, and for none of them to become a hidden blocker. The more you balance attention strategically, the more allies you create and the more effectively you build buy-in across the customer organization.

> **Pro Tip: Multi-Thread Without Undermining Trust**
>
> It's smart to build relationships beyond your main contact, but only if you can do it without undermining them. Multi-threading can deepen your influence and reduce risk if your primary contact leaves, but done carelessly, it can damage trust. Always loop in your contact, give them credit, and position them as the point of coordination. When in doubt, ask: *"Would it be helpful if I connected with [name] directly, or would you prefer to make that introduction?"* Tread lightly. One strong relationship is better than five shaky ones.

Shift 3 – Spreading Your Influence

Group meetings provide an opportunity to expand your influence within the customer organization. A junior team member today may be your main point of contact tomorrow. A peer or manager could be a powerful advocate... or a hidden blocker. Take the opportunity to engage with and make a positive impression on everyone in the room.

The more people who know you, trust you, and feel heard by you, the more resilient your account becomes.

Shift 4 – Elevating Your Primary Contact

Your job isn't just to accomplish your goals within the meeting, it's to do so in a way that elevates your primary contact at the same time.

Whenever possible, highlight their contributions. Share how they helped prepare, cleared internal roadblocks, or advocated for the initiative you're there to discuss. Done well, these moments strengthen your internal champion, build trust, and signal that you're a partner, not just a vendor.

Just be sure your praise is authentic, not performative. Overdoing it will feel like flattery and hurt your credibility. But a sincere comment, dropped into the right moment, can go a long way.

I remember reviewing the early results of a complex rollout with my primary contact and her manager. The project had been bumpy, and frankly, it wouldn't have succeeded without her help navigating internal systems and smoothing out the handoffs. So when I walked through the numbers, I made a point to say, *"A lot of this came together because Denise really pushed things forward behind the scenes. There were a few spots where we might've gotten stuck, but she kept everything moving."*

Her manager nodded, took a note, and smiled. After the meeting, my contact pulled me aside and said, *"Thank you for saying that. It really meant something coming from you."*

The key isn't to steal attention or try to win favor, it's to shine a light on the person who's been helping you succeed. When your contact looks good in front of their team or leadership, you deepen the relationship and increase your ability to get things done together going forward.

Common Pitfalls in One-to-One and Small Group Meetings

Even seasoned account managers can stumble in the room. Small mistakes can have a big impact in close settings. Stay present, flexible, and aware, and your in-person meetings will stand out for the right reasons. Here are a few mistakes to watch out for.

Pitfall 1 – Being Underprepared
Don't wing it. In-person time is valuable; bring a plan, not just presence.

Pitfall 2 – Talking Too Much
It's a meeting, not a monologue. Leave space for dialogue, especially in small groups.

Pitfall 3 – Ignoring Body Language
You're in the room, so read the room. Look for cues and adjust in real time.

Pitfall 4 – Over-Relying on Slides
Keep visuals simple and secondary. The real presentation is *you*.

Pitfall 5 – Focusing Only on the Decision Maker
In small groups, ignoring other voices can cost you quiet allies.

Avoid these missteps, and you'll turn good meetings into great ones — and great ones into long-term momentum.

Putting it All Together
One-to-one and small group meetings follow the same playbook, but they call for a few different moves. Here's a quick side-by-side to help you spot the difference and show up ready for both.

Quick Guide: One-to-One vs. Small Group Meetings		
	One-to-One	**Small Group**
Primary Focus	Depth of relationship and individual alignment	Group consensus and collective momentum
Dynamic	Intimate, personal	Complex, multi-stakeholder
Preparation Tip	Personalize agenda and goals	Align on roles, introductions, and power dynamics
Conversation Style	Dialogue with one decision-maker	Dialogue + facilitation across participants
Attention Strategy	Focus on the individual	Balance focus across group members
Pitfall to Avoid	Being too casual or unstructured	Ignoring side participants or hidden blockers

Final Thought

Great meetings don't happen by accident. They happen because you showed up prepared, read the room, and made the time matter. If you can do that consistently, you won't just run meetings; you'll lead them.

Chapter 6 Recap

Key Takeaways

- One-to-one meetings build trust.
- Small group meetings drive decisions.
- Both formats require preparation, presence, and an ability to adapt to personalities in the room.

Reflection Questions

- Are you creating space for real dialogue in your meetings or just running through a checklist?
- In small groups, how do you balance your attention without losing focus?
- What's one small habit you can adopt to improve your presence during in-person conversations?

Apply It Now

- Create an agenda for a one-to-one meeting. Leave space for both relationship-building and results.
- In your next group setting, even outside of work, practice spreading your attention. Be deliberate about including everyone.

Chapter 7

One-to-Many Meetings

I once spent an entire day talking about disinfectant wipes. Eight back-to-back sessions. Same message, same product, same talking points delivered again and again to rotating groups of sales reps at a customer event. By the end of the day, I was completely drained.

But something surprising happened. My last session? It was the best one. I had refined my delivery, sharpened my message, and figured out exactly what landed with the audience. And over the next few weeks, I saw a solid lift in sales. The reps had clearly taken the message to heart and taken it to their buyers.

What I accomplished in that one day would've taken months through one-to-one meetings. That's the power of one-to-many. It's fast, focused, and scalable… if you know how to make the most of it.

In one-to-many meetings, your role shifts from relationship-builder to message-broadcaster. You're not there for a conversation. You're there to command the room, deliver a clear message, and leave a lasting impression. Whether you're on stage at a conference, rotating through breakout sessions, or pitching from a trade show booth, the goal is the same: deliver a message that sticks.

In this chapter, we'll break down the three most common one-to-many formats:

1. **Main Stage Presentations**
2. **Round-Robin Sessions**
3. **Trade Show Meetings**

Each meeting type calls for a different approach. Let's look at how to prep, perform, and deliver impact at scale, no matter what type of room you're in.

– A Crash Course in Main Stage Presentations –

Main stage meetings are your moment in the spotlight. Whether you're speaking to ten people or ten thousand, a main stage presentation puts you front and center. It's your job to inform, engage, and leave a lasting impression, often without much real-time feedback.

Part 1 – Before the Meeting

Main stage sessions are high-stakes and highly visible. You'll be addressing a room full of people who are expecting value, so thorough preparation is a must.

- **Understand your audience.** Are they experts in your field or complete newcomers? Tailor your content accordingly.
- **Clarify logistics.** Ask about tech (mic type, slide clicker, screen layout), your time slot, and any content themes.
- **Know your role.** Are you the keynote, part of a series, or closing the event? Adjust your tone and content to fit your role.
- **Design for delivery.** Build a clean and visually appealing presentation that supports your story without overwhelming the audience.

> **Pro Tip: Cater to Your Audience**
>
> If you're addressing a room full of retail buyers, avoid technical jargon. Highlight use cases, customer impact, and quick wins. But if you're speaking to product engineers, go deeper into the mechanics of how your product works.

Part 2 – Arrival and Set Up

Arrive early, ideally the day before, to walk the stage, test the tech, and rehearse in the room where you'll present.

- Check your slides on the actual display system.
- Walk the space: Know where you'll stand, how far your voice carries, and which areas to avoid blocking.
- Confirm timing and agenda with the organizer to avoid surprises.

Part 3 – Introductions and Opening

You're the show. So, open strong.

- Introduce yourself briefly but memorably. Share why you're credible and relatable.
- Hook the audience with a story, a question, or a compelling stat.
- Preview what's coming. Tease your core message.

Example:

"I once spent 15 hours fixing a supply chain issue for a product that sold out in two days. I'll tell you how we fixed it, and how you can avoid running into the same issue."

Part 4 – The Presentation

This is a performance. Energy, pacing, and presence matter.

- Use the whole stage. Move with purpose, avoid aimless pacing.
- Make eye contact with all areas of the room.
- Vary your tone. Emphasize key points with pauses or volume changes.
- Don't just deliver info, tell a story.

Part 5 – Closing the Meeting

End with impact. Leave your audience ready to take action.

- Summarize your main points.
- Reinforce your call to action. Make your ask clear so your audience knows what you want them to do next.
- Leave them with a quote, a story, or a challenge they won't forget.

– A Crash Course in Round-Robin Sessions –

Round robins are your endurance test. You'll deliver the same presentation multiple times to rotating groups. The key? Keep your energy up, your message sharp, and your delivery fresh every time.

Part 1 – Before the Meeting

Round-robin sessions demand strategic planning and repeatable performance. You'll need a message that stays sharp through repetition — consistent, but never stale.

- Plan a concise and engaging presentation (10–15 minutes maximum).
- Align with any event themes (e.g., wellness, sustainability), even if you can only do so loosely.
- Include interactive elements to re-energize each group.

Example:

If the theme is "Future of Work" and you sell ergonomic office chairs, tailor your pitch to how your product improves remote productivity.

Part 2 – Arrival and Set Up

Arrive early to:

- Learn the schedule so you know your break times and the number of rotations.
- Test the tech in each room, or understand how you'll transport your materials.
- Prep your space: Set up product samples, handouts, or props.

Part 3 - Introductions and Opening

Keep it tight:

- State your name, company, and share one unique or fun fact.
- Hook them with a question or visual to grab their attention right away.

Example:

"How many of you sat in three back-to-back meetings this morning? What if your chair actually helped you focus instead of hurting your back?"

Part 4 - The Presentation

You'll be repeating yourself, but it doesn't need to sound like it.

- Stay animated and fresh for each group.
- Adjust on the fly. If something worked well with the previous group, use it again. If something fell flat, cut it.
- Involve the audience. Use raised hands, informal polls, or direct questions.

Part 5 - Closing the Meeting

Don't let the session fizzle out just because people are watching the clock.

- Reiterate your takeaway message early, don't save it for the end.

- Use the final minutes for Q&A or an interactive wrap-up.
- Always end on time, or even a minute early.

– A Crash Course in Trade Show Booth Meetings –

Trade shows are your agility test. They are organized chaos, like giving a product demo in the middle of an airport terminal. You can't control who walks up or how long they stay, but you can control the experience they have. Your challenge is to deliver a compelling message, quickly and frequently, in an unpredictable environment.

Part 1 – Before the Meeting

Trade shows are fast-paced and random. Prepare for a free-for-all.

- Develop a short, flexible pitch (1–3 minutes).
- Know your product inside and out, you won't have slides to fall back on.
- Bring samples, props, or handouts that draw attention.

Example:

If you're selling flavored protein drinks, set out sample cups for people to try. Lead with something like, "Want to taste something that converted 80% of first-time samplers?"

Part 2 – Arrival and Set Up

Trade shows are all about showmanship.

- Arrive early to set up, often the day before.
- Set up your booth for visual impact: use clear signage, maintain a clean layout, and incorporate attention-grabbing elements.
- Make sure you have giveaways. People stop for swag, but they stay for substance.

Part 3 – Introductions and Opening

Keep it light and friendly.

- Greet attendees by name if you can read their badge.
- Ask simple questions like: "What's been your favorite booth so far?"
- Attention spans are short, so transition quickly into your presentation and pitch.

Part 4 – The Presentation

Keep it quick and flexible:

- Start from anywhere, beginning, middle, or end, depending on when someone walks up.

- Watch for cues. If someone's engaged, go deeper. If they're glancing around, wrap it up.
- If a new person joins, greet them and either restart or catch them up quickly.
- Incorporate your pitch early and often.

Part 5 – Closing the Meeting

Trade shows don't have formal goodbyes.

- Offer a call to action: "Would you like a sample?" or "Want to schedule a follow-up?"
- Thank them for stopping by and offer a branded item or business card.
- Be ready to shift gears instantly when the next person walks up.

Trade shows might be unpredictable, but they're one of the best opportunities to scale exposure, spark curiosity, and generate quick leads — if you're able to make the most of them.

Common Pitfalls in One-to-Many Meetings

One-to-many formats can be high-reward, but only if you avoid the missteps that can dull your message or cause you to lose the room. Since one-to-many formats leave less room for recovery, let's review some common pitfalls to avoid. Here are some of the most common traps, and how to steer clear of them:

Pitfall 1 – Talking At, Not To Your Audience

When you're addressing a crowd, it's easy to slip into broadcast mode. But even large audiences want to feel spoken to, not spoken at. Use inclusive language ("you" instead of "they"), ask rhetorical questions, and make eye contact, even if it's across a sea of faces.

Pitfall 2 – Overloading Your Slides

Slides should support your story, not compete with it. Too much text, tiny fonts, or cluttered visuals draw attention away from you and confuse your message. Aim for clarity. One idea per slide. Simple visuals. Big, bold fonts.

Pitfall 3 – Ignoring the Room's Energy

If the audience looks confused, distracted, or restless, don't plow ahead like nothing's happening. Adjust. Slow down. Reframe a key point. Ask a question. Great presenters read the room and respond in real time.

Pitfall 4 – Letting Q&A Drag On

Whether on stage or in a round-robin session, ending with an unstructured Q&A can derail a strong finish. Set time limits. Have a closing line ready and if questions go long, offer to follow up afterward.

Pitfall 5 – Repeating Without Re-Energizing

In round-robin formats, it's easy to go on autopilot. But the tenth group deserves the same energy and clarity as the first. Reset between sessions. If you're bored with your own pitch, your audience definitely will be.

Putting it All Together

All one-to-many meetings scale your message, but each format comes with its own dynamics. Here's a quick side-by-side to help you tailor your approach to the room you're walking into.

Quick Guide: One-to-Many Meetings			
	Main Stage	**Round-Robin**	**Trade Show**
Primary Goal	Inspire and inform a large audience	Deliver a pitch to small rotating groups	Capture attention and generate leads in real-time
Audience Size	Large (dozens to thousands)	Small (5–15 per session)	Unpredictable foot traffic
Interaction Level	Low – mostly one-way communication	Medium – some interaction, repeatable script	High – informal, quick back-and-forth
Prep Focus	Presentation flow and stage presence	Message clarity and delivery endurance	Flexible pitch and fast reactions
Energy Required	Performance-level presence	Endurance and consistency	Adaptability and alertness

Final Thought

When you're presenting at scale, avoiding these pitfalls can be the difference between being remembered and being forgotten. Not every meeting happens in a room or on a stage. More often, you're presenting from behind a screen, where it's even harder to hold attention and build a connection.

And that's exactly where we're headed next: the world of virtual meetings.

Chapter 7 Recap

Key Takeaways

- One-to-many meetings require clarity, consistency, and confidence.
- These formats aren't about back-and-forth conversation; they're about commanding attention.
- Your delivery, energy, and message need to be tailored for scale.

Reflection Questions

- How can you make your next presentation more engaging, even with a silent audience?
- Are you using body language and tone effectively to command attention?

Apply It Now

- Record yourself delivering a 2-minute pitch. Watch it. Does it land? Would you be intrigued?
- Build a checklist for each type of one-to-many meeting you might encounter. Include items like preparation, technology, messaging, and follow-up.

Chapter 8

Virtual Meetings

One day, I met with ten different customers without ever leaving my desk.

Ten virtual meetings. Back-to-back. Some quick check-ins, some full presentations. I also cleared out my inbox, handled a few internal escalations, and even wrapped up my admin work early. It was one of my most productive days of the quarter.

How? No traffic. No flights. No walking across parking lots or waiting in lobbies. Just one meeting after another, separated by nothing but the click of a "Join" button.

That's the power of virtual meetings: speed, scale, and efficiency.

But there's a flip side. Without face-to-face connection, it's harder to read the room, build trust, or recover from a misstep. You have less time, less presence, and far less margin for error.

To succeed, you need to become part host, part producer — intentionally crafting every detail, from the agenda and visuals to your tone and lighting.

This chapter will show you how to turn virtual meetings into high-impact moments that build credibility, deepen relationships, and drive results.

- A Crash Course in Virtual Meetings -

Great virtual meetings don't happen by accident. They're built step by step from the invite to the wrap-up. Here's how to make every detail count, even from behind a screen.

Part 1 – Before the Meeting: Think Like a Producer

Every great virtual meeting starts *before* anyone clicks "Join."

- Use your customer's preferred platform (e.g., Zoom, Teams, Google Meet). Creating a friction-free experience for your customer starts with using what's familiar.
- Send a calendar invite with the link, time zone clarity, attendee names, and a clear agenda.

- Prep your content like a professional. Know what you'll say, what you'll show, and how you'll pivot if things change.

Virtual meetings strip away the charm of small talk at the door or the ambiance of a boardroom. That means every detail you control, from the agenda to the visuals, carries extra weight.

Part 2 – Logging On: Set the Right Tone

Showing up late to a virtual meeting isn't just inconvenient; it's disruptive. It signals disorganization and disinterest.

- If possible, join 3–5 minutes early to resolve issues before customers arrive.
- Test your camera, microphone, and screen sharing capabilities, especially if it's a new platform.
- Mute your mic immediately upon entry, then unmute only when speaking.

I once joined a VP's kickoff call exactly as they started speaking, only to realize I'd forgotten to mute myself. That very moment, my doorbell rang, and my dog started barking, giving everyone an unplanned sound check of me shushing her. I apologized, quipped, "I guess my dog really wanted to join the call today!" and we all laughed. It loosened the room, but I always mute on entry now.

Being early, smooth, and stable creates immediate confidence. It tells your customer: "You can count on me."

Part 3 - Opening the Meeting: Building Rapport from a Distance

Digital rapport takes more than a smile. Without shared space, small gestures carry more significance.

- Use names. Reintroduce yourself and others if needed.
- Lean into warm openers. Try "How's your week been?" or "What's new on your end?"
- Mirror your customer's tone. If they're buttoned-up, match their pace and language. If they're relaxed, allow yourself to be more conversational.

The goal is to humanize the interaction quickly. Start building trust in the first 90 seconds, not 90 minutes.

Part 4 - Leading the Meeting: Facilitate with Intention

As the account manager, you're still the host, even from behind a webcam.

- **State the agenda clearly up front.** Let them know where you're going and how you'll get there.
- **Use pauses intentionally.** Let silence breathe. Ask open-ended questions. Invite participation with prompts like "I'd love your take on this" or "What's your reaction to that so far?"
- **Treat every participant with respect.** Virtual meetings often include junior team members or silent

observers. Today's listener could be tomorrow's decision-maker.
- **Watch for engagement cues.** A tilted head, a pause, or a furrowed brow might be the only signal you get that someone has a question.

I once noticed a customer's eyebrows shoot up as I scrolled to a pricing slide. I paused and simply asked, "Did something stand out there?" That one question opened a key conversation about budget alignment that would have gone unnoticed if I'd kept moving.

Great virtual hosts don't just share slides; they guide the conversation. When you facilitate with intention, every click feels personal, and every attendee feels heard.

Part 5 - Mastering Tech and Timing

In virtual meetings, things will go wrong and energy will fade if you don't manage them actively.

- **If something fails, pivot quickly.** Don't freeze or disappear. Most platforms have a dial-in number. When in doubt, call in. Customers would rather hear your voice without video than sit in silence.
- **Have a backup plan.** A hotspot, alternate link, or second device can save a meeting.

- **Bring energy.** Virtual meetings are efficient, but back-to-back calls can be draining. Remember, you're not just presenting, you're managing the customer's focus.
- **Honor the clock.** Just because everyone's remote doesn't mean they have more time to spare. If you're running long, say so and give the customer the option to continue or reschedule.

Glitches happen, attention drifts, and clocks keep ticking. Your calm pivot — and respect for their time — turns potential chaos into confidence.

Part 6 – Leverage Built-In Virtual Tools

Today's video platforms give you more than just "face time," they have features you can use to drive engagement, gather feedback, and co-create in real time.

- **Use screen annotations and shared whiteboards.** Sketch live diagrams, highlight key data on your slides, or let attendees drop virtual "sticky notes" with their ideas.
- **Tap the chat for real-time input.** Invite participants to post blockers, questions, or quick wins, then address them immediately instead of waiting.
- **Run a chat poll.** Ask relevant questions to get instant group alignment and see priorities surface in seconds.

- **Split larger groups into breakout rooms.** Give small teams 5–10 minutes to brainstorm, then reconvene and have each group share their top insights.

I once led a quarterly business review entirely over Teams, and instead of just talking through slides, I embedded a two-question live poll in the chat: "Which outcome matters most?" and "What's our biggest roadblock?"

Within seconds, six participants voted and commented. One director messaged afterward, *"I've never felt this engaged in a virtual meeting, this was more like a workshop than a presentation."*

That simple poll not only broke the ice but also directly shaped our action plan on the spot. We wrapped up with clear, co-created next steps, and they signed off on an expansion before the week was out.

Virtual tools aren't just bells and whistles; they're bridges. Use them wisely, and your meetings shift from passive viewing to active participation.

Part 7 – Closing with Confidence

Wrap your meetings the way pros land planes: clearly, smoothly, and with forward momentum.

- Summarize key takeaways.
- Confirm next steps, including owners and deadlines.
- Schedule your next meeting before ending the call.

- End warmly, with appreciation and a clear exit: "Thanks for your time today. I'll send a follow-up summary shortly, and we're on for next Thursday."

Leave them with clarity, not confusion. And always follow through on any plans made during the meeting.

Pro Tip: Maintaining Momentum

Scheduling a meeting over email often leads to delays or missed follow-ups. Before ending a virtual meeting, pull up calendars and book the next one on the spot. It's faster, easier, and keeps the momentum going without extra back-and-forth. A confirmed next step shows progress and keeps things moving.

Core Skills for Virtual Meetings

To succeed in a virtual meeting, you'll need all the foundational skills from in-person meetings, plus a few more that are specific to working behind a screen. These four skills are the difference between showing up and standing out in a virtual environment.

Skill 1 – Presence

Your physical presence is limited, so your digital presence must be *felt*.

- Dress for the role, from the waist up.
    - Shorts and slippers are fine, just keep them off camera!
- Light yourself clearly. Position your camera at eye level.
- Choose a background that's professional *and* personal (sports memorabilia, plants, books, or anything else that invites conversation).

In most industries, a fun or personality-filled background can be a great way to connect, as long as it's intentional. For example, I have my bobblehead collection and some other sports memorabilia behind me in my office. This is intentional as it often gives me something to talk about with my customers. Whether they recognize the team name on a helmet or ask, "What's with all the bobbleheads?" I'm ready to respond and use the opening to begin creating a connection with my customer.

Showcase your personality, but keep it relevant and audience-aware. A sports-themed background or a short story is great, just be careful not to dominate the meeting with personal anecdotes that your customer can't relate to.

Skill 2 – Preparedness

In a virtual world, there's no room for "winging it."

- Have slides, notes, and supporting docs open and organized.
- Practice screen sharing before the meeting.
- Rehearse how you'll navigate your presentation and any other content you plan to share.

Preparedness isn't about having more material. It's about being ready to deliver it smoothly and confidently.

Skill 3 – Presenting Virtually

When you're presenting virtually, your slides and your voice need to do the heavy lifting. You may be reduced to a small box or even disappear altogether if someone pins the presentation.

To make your delivery count:

- Show energy through voice and facial expression.
- Make eye contact with the camera (not just your screen).
- Tell a quick personal story or joke if the moment is right.

The goal is to make the meeting feel *alive*, not like another slide deck in a long, gray day.

If you're sharing your screen, close anything you wouldn't want customers to see. Stay on one app unless switching is intentional. Use dual monitors when possible, one for presenting, one for watching faces. This helps you stay connected while sharing your screen.

Avoid the mistake I once made where I was double-checking my travel plans for an upcoming trip while still broadcasting my screen. Thankfully, the travel plans were for a visit with the customer I was talking to, and they understood and we brushed it off with a joke. However, it was an awkward moment and could have left my customer feeling like I wasn't fully invested in the meeting.

Skill 4 – Flexibility and Digital Showmanship

Virtual meetings are dynamic. Things go wrong. Attention spans wander. That's why you need to be able to pivot on the fly.

- If your deck isn't landing, pivot to something else, like a product demo.
- If a question comes up, be ready to Google it live via screen share or draw a diagram to work through it with your customer.
- If your tech fails, have a backup plan.

I once lost Wi-Fi mid-pitch, but I jumped onto a hotspot and was back online in under a minute. That recovery impressed the customer more than a perfect demo would have.

Being resourceful builds credibility. Adaptability wins business. If you can shift gears without missing a beat, you'll stand out.

Common Pitfalls in Virtual Meetings

Even experienced account managers can fall into traps that weaken virtual meetings. Here are a few to avoid:

Pitfall 1 – Failing to Engage Visually

If your camera is off or your background is distracting, you'll lose credibility quickly.

Pitfall 2 – Overreliance on Slides

Don't let your visuals do all the talking. Your voice and personality still matter.

Pitfall 3 – Tech Stumble

Don't share your screen until you're ready. Test before meetings. Know how to switch audio sources or join by phone.

Pitfall 4 – Skipping the Soft Open

Going straight into business feels cold. Virtual rapport needs deliberate warmth.

Pitfall 5 – Dragging On Past Time

It's easier to lose track remotely. Watch the clock and always ask before running over.

Putting it All Together

You've seen the steps, skills, and potential pitfalls. Now here's a quick-reference guide to help you pull it all together. Use this blueprint to plan, run, and follow up on virtual meetings that feel seamless, purposeful, and professional — every time.

Virtual Meeting Blueprint	
Stage	**What to Do**
Before the Meeting	- Use the customer's preferred platform - Send agenda & link in invite - Prep your content
Logging On	- Join 3–5 min early - Test tech - Mute on entry
Opening the Meeting	- Greet by name - Warm opener - Mirror tone
Leading the Meeting	- Share agenda up front - Ask questions - Watch for visual cues
Managing Tech and Time	- Have a backup plan - Keep energy up - Respect time limits
Using Virtual Tools	- Whiteboards - Polls - Breakout rooms
Closing with Confidence	- Recap takeaways - Confirm next steps - Book the next meeting

Final Thought

Virtual meetings aren't just a stopgap until you can meet in person; they're a core part of modern account management. And they aren't just the new normal either. They're a new advantage for those who know how to use them.

When you treat virtual meetings with the same care you'd give an in-person meeting, you turn every screen into an opportunity to build trust, spark collaboration, and drive results. Mastering these digital dynamics today will set you apart tomorrow, no matter where or how you meet your customers.

Chapter 8 Recap

Key Takeaways

- Virtual meetings make your calendar more efficient, but also more demanding.
- Your voice, visuals, and virtual presence all need to work harder than they do in person.
- Technology will fail. Your ability to pivot quickly will define your success.

Reflection Questions

- What's your plan when tech breaks mid-meeting?
- What does your background say about you? Is there anything you can change to make it say what you want it to say?

Apply It Now

- Run a full mock virtual meeting. Check your lighting, background, audio, and platform connectivity all at once.
- Practice joining different conferencing platforms. If you run into issues with any, figure out how to resolve them.

Chapter 9

Listening and Responding

I once had a customer who barely said a word for the first six months of our relationship. Every meeting felt transactional, just quick updates and short answers. I thought they were disengaged.

But during one quarterly review, I decided to change my approach. Instead of leading with updates or recommendations, I asked a simple question: "What's something we could be doing better for you?"

There was a pause. Then they said, *"To be honest, it's hard to tell where things stand. We get updates, but we're not always sure what they mean for us or what to focus on."*

That one comment shifted everything. It wasn't that they were disengaged; they didn't feel heard. From that moment on, I started every call by asking what was on their mind. I shared more context. I stopped assuming and started listening.

Within a quarter, the relationship went from cold to collaborative. They invited us into more strategic conversations and eventually expanded their investment significantly.

It wasn't a new product or flashy pitch that changed the trajectory. It was better listening.

Listening isn't passive; it's one of your most active tools as an account manager. When you truly listen and respond with care, you build trust, deepen relationships, and position yourself to win.

Whether you're in a meeting, on a call, or exchanging emails, every conversation is an opportunity to uncover what your customer really needs. But to capture those insights, you can't just wait for your turn to speak. You have to listen with purpose. That means hearing their words, reading between the lines, and responding in ways that show you understand.

When you listen intentionally, your meetings stop feeling like pitches and start sounding like real conversations. The kind that take you off-script and require real-time thinking. Unlike a practiced pitch, conversations require you to think on your feet, a skill that improves with practice and preparation.

Conversations open the door to questions. Questions open the door to insights and objections, both of which lead to a deeper understanding of your customer's needs. This understanding is what enables you to build successful, long-term relationships while making sales without selling.

– A Crash Course in Effective Listening –

Key 1 – Give Your Customer a Chance to Speak

Listening starts with space. If you dominate the conversation, especially in one-to-one or small group settings, your customer won't have the chance to speak, and you'll miss what they're trying to tell you.

Avoid turning every meeting into a monologue. Instead, build in natural pauses, even during presentations. Try planning in questions like:

- "Does that make sense so far?"
- "Any thoughts or questions?"
- "Is this tracking with your priorities?"

This not only encourages engagement but also creates a more collaborative dynamic, transforming your message from a presentation into a conversation.

Key 2 – Take the Time to Truly Listen

It's easy to fall into "pitch mode" and rush through your talking points while missing what your customer is actually telling you. But true listening requires focusing with intention. Don't plan what you'll say on your next slide while they're still speaking.

Tune in to what they're saying and think about why they are saying it.

I learned this the hard way.

Early in a customer meeting, I was asked a question. Eager to stick to my plan, I brushed it off with, *"We'll cover that later,"* and kept going. When I finished the deck, I expected enthusiasm. Instead, I received frustration.

The customer repeated their question, one I now realized I hadn't actually answered. Worse, I couldn't even recall what it was they had asked until it was repeated. When they asked it again, the answer was straightforward, but it hadn't been covered in my presentation, and I didn't address it like I'd said I would.

Had I paused and truly listened, I could have pivoted, tailored the presentation to ensure it answered their question, and likely uncovered a major opportunity. Instead, I had to apologize and ask for a second chance.

Thankfully, I got one. But you won't always. That's why real listening matters, because if you miss what your customer is really asking, no presentation can save you.

Key 3 - Repeat the Question Your Customer Asks

When your customer asks a question, repeat it back before answering.

- "Just to confirm, you're asking if we offer monthly billing options?"
- "Let me make sure I understand. You're wondering if we can integrate with your internal tools?"

This accomplishes three things:
1. It shows that you're actively listening.
2. It buys you a moment to think.
3. It gives the customer a chance to clarify or even answer the question themselves.

It's a simple habit with a big upside and no downside.

Pro Tip: "Go Deaf" (Strategically)

If a question catches you off guard or you're unsure how to respond, try this:

"I want to make sure I caught that. Would you mind repeating it?"

Most customers will naturally rephrase or add context, giving you more to work with. You haven't stalled, you've created space. And often, that second version is clearer, more specific, or easier to respond to. It's a simple move that can turn a tough moment into a better answer.

Key 4 - Focus on More than Just the Words

Words matter. But tone, posture, and expression often reveal more than what's said.

Watch for signs of alignment or misalignment:

- Do they say they're "interested," but sit back with folded arms and minimal eye contact?
- Do they claim to be "not convinced," but lean in with eager body language?

When you spot discrepancies between words and behavior, take note. That's your cue to ask a follow-up question. Something like:

- "I noticed you didn't seem super excited about that last point. Do you want me to try explaining it better?"

Visual and vocal cues provide valuable insights into what your customer is really thinking. Pay attention to everything.

This is especially important in virtual settings where nonverbal cues are limited. Even subtle expressions, such as a raised eyebrow, a hesitant pause, or an extended silence, might be your cue to slow down, ask a clarifying question, and make sure you are aligned.

Key 5 – Learn to Recognize an Objection

Not every question or statement is benign. Some are objections in disguise.

Customers rarely present their full reasoning upfront. Objections are often the tip of the iceberg, so your goal is to get below the surface and understand what's really stopping them.

Your job is to recognize when a statement represents a barrier, not just curiosity. An objection may sound like:

- "We've tried something like this before, and it didn't work."
- "That sounds great, but it's probably out of our budget."

These aren't just passing comments, they're signals.

Don't jump in with a canned response. Instead:

1. Pause.
2. Ask follow-up questions.
3. Understand the true root of the objection.

Once you do, you'll be positioned to respond more effectively and more persuasively.

Key 6 - Unpack Objections

When a customer raises a concern, don't jump straight to solving it. Start by understanding it.

Objections usually signal deeper concerns, like past failures, internal friction, or financial pressure. But customers rarely say all of that outright. Your job is to unpack what's really going on.

Ask follow-up questions like:

- "Can you tell me more about what happened last time?"
- "When you say it's a timing concern, is that about bandwidth or budget cycles?"
- "What would success look like on your end?"

Treat objections as openings, not obstacles. When you slow down and show curiosity, you turn tension into trust and gain the clarity you need to respond well.

Once you've unpacked the objection, you'll be ready to respond with clarity and confidence.

> **Pro Tip: Objections Aren't Roadblocks, They're Road Signs**
>
> They tell you where your customer is uncertain, hesitant, or unconvinced. Don't avoid them. Navigate through them.

Listening isn't just about being quiet; it's about being tuned in. When you give your customer room to speak, focus fully on what they're saying (and not saying), and recognize when a question is really an objection, you unlock what they actually need.

Now that you know how to listen effectively, let's talk about how to respond in ways that build trust, address concerns, and move the conversation forward.

– A Crash Course in Responding with Impact –

Great responses follow a simple rhythm: **Listen. Think. Respond.**

Step 1 – <u>Listen</u> First

You can't respond effectively if you don't understand the question or the concern behind it. Before you respond, be sure you've really understood the question. Not just the words, but the tone and intent behind them. Everything you say next depends on that clarity.

And if you miss the mark? You may create confusion, or worse, erode trust.

I was in a quarterly review with a customer when they asked, *"How flexible is your platform?"*

I launched into a full explanation of our integration options, thinking they were asking about technical capabilities. But a few minutes in, the customer interrupted and said, *"Sorry, I meant contract flexibility. We've had to scale our usage up and down a lot this year."*

I'd answered confidently, just not to the question they were actually asking.

I paused, owned the miss, and said, *"Thanks for clarifying. That's really helpful context. Let me walk you through how we handle volume changes."*

The conversation recovered, but it reminded me that the first step to a great answer is making sure you know what's really being asked. Had I slowed down and clarified at the start, I could've answered the *right* question the first time.

Step 2 – Take the Time You Need to Think

Not every question needs an instant answer. And trying to respond too quickly, especially when you're unsure, can backfire.

Instead, restate or clarify the question to buy yourself a moment and show you're thinking carefully, not stalling.

- Or be direct and say something like: "That's a great question. Do you mind if I take a minute to think it through?"

- Or if you truly don't know, say something like: "I want to make sure I give you the right information. Let me dig into that and follow up."

Customers will respect your honesty and your follow-up. Just make sure you actually follow up and do so promptly.

> **Pro Tip: Pause, Parrot, Proceed**
>
> When you get a tough question, pause. Restate it to confirm. Then respond with intention, even if that response is, "Let me follow up." This pattern buys you time and shows composure under pressure.

Step 3 – <u>Respond</u> with Clarity and Confidence

Once you've unpacked the objection or fully understood the question, it's time to respond clearly, completely, and with purpose.

Great responses do two things:

1. They answer the question honestly.
2. They reinforce your value.

You don't have to dodge tough topics or over-explain shortcomings. Just tell the truth in a way that builds confidence.

If you're missing a requested feature:

- Acknowledge the gap.
- Share what you do offer and why our approach often works better for customers with similar goals.

Example:
"You're right, we don't have that exact feature. But here's what we do offer instead, and why some of our customers prefer it."

This kind of response signals credibility and strategic thinking. You're not spinning; you're guiding. And when your answers are thoughtful and aligned with what matters to the customer, they carry weight.

Once you master the art of listening and learn how to respond with intent, you stop playing catch-up and start leading the conversation.

Final Thought

When you listen with intention and respond with clarity, you shift the dynamic. You stop reacting and start guiding. You earn credibility not with perfect answers, but with thoughtful ones. The kind that prove you're paying attention and that you genuinely understand what matters most.

That's when customers start bringing you into bigger conversations. Not because you sell something, but because they trust you to help them make the right call.

The customer who once gave one-word answers? They're now a strategic partner. All because I stopped pitching and started listening.

Chapter 9 Recap

Key Takeaways

- Listening is about more than hearing. It's about reading tone, intent, and unspoken concerns.
- Your responses carry weight. Use them to clarify, persuade, and deepen trust.
- Objections are opportunities. They give you a chance to go deeper and guide the conversation forward.

Reflection Questions

- Have you ever responded too quickly and missed what your customer was really asking?
- Think of a time a customer raised a concern. Did you explore it fully before responding?

Apply It Now

- On your next customer call, ask three follow-up questions and pause after each to fully absorb the response.
- Practice saying, "That's a great question. Let me get back to you on that," out loud. Say it until it feels comfortable, then use it whenever you're unsure how to answer a question.

Chapter 10

Relationship Building

Not long ago, I was presenting to a large group of prospective customers, walking through an analysis my team offers — one that identifies cost-saving opportunities and helps customers drive adoption. The content was solid. My delivery was clear. But the room? Quiet. Polite nods, but not much energy. It felt like the value just wasn't landing.

Then something changed.

One of my longtime customers, seated near the front, raised her hand.

"Bill ran this exact analysis for me and it led to a 15% cost reduction. It also helped us become way more efficient with adoption. I highly recommend it."

That one comment flipped the room. Heads lifted. Laptops closed. Suddenly, everyone wanted to know more about the analysis, how it worked, and how soon they could get one too.

Later that day, I pulled her aside to say thank you. Her response stuck with me:

"I could tell they weren't getting it, but I've seen firsthand the value you bring. Don't worry, I've got your back whenever you need me."

That's the power of relationships. They don't just help you serve a customer; they create *advocates*. People who speak up when you're not in the room. People who help you cut through the noise and earn credibility before you've said a word. Relationships like that can't be faked or fast-tracked; they're built through trust, consistency, and shared success over time.

The ability to build trust and rapport quickly and confidently is a defining trait of high-performing account managers.

In account management, long-term relationships matter more than short-term wins. Strong customer relationships lead to more honest communication, smoother negotiations, and better sales outcomes. They give you an edge when your product or price isn't the best on paper, because customers don't just buy from companies; they buy from people they trust.

There's a common misconception that great relationships are built simply through time and familiarity. While time *helps*, it isn't what earns trust. Effort does. Some account managers work with the same contacts for years and never build more than surface-level rapport. Others walk into a new account and build trust within weeks.

The difference is intention.

Strong relationships don't happen by accident. They're built through clear communication, small moments of reliability, and consistent follow-through. Whether you're working with a single point of contact or managing a rotating cast of stakeholders, your ability to build meaningful, durable relationships will define your long-term success.

Because at the end of the day, a strong relationship doesn't just help you win *with* your customer, it helps you grow *beyond* them.

– A Crash Course in Relationship Building –

Strong relationships aren't built through one big moment, they're built through consistent actions over time. The steps that follow will help you do just that.

Step 1 – Put Your Customer First

One of the fastest ways to build trust is to prioritize your customer's goals alongside your own. That doesn't mean forgetting about your sales target, it means understanding that your success depends on theirs.

Put yourself in your customer's shoes. What are they measured on? What are their priorities? What challenges might they be facing behind the scenes that haven't yet surfaced in conversation?

If you can show them that your goals are aligned with theirs and that your value comes from helping them hit their goals, you move from "vendor" to "strategic partner." That's a relationship no competitor can easily replace.

This doesn't mean saying "yes" to everything or letting the customer walk all over you. A truly customer-first mindset is about balance, finding ways to deliver value to the customer while protecting your ability to deliver results for your own company.

> **Pro Tip: Make Their Win Your Win**
>
> If you've closed the deal, you're already winning. Now the real work begins, proving your value. The best account managers treat every interaction as an opportunity to deliver outcomes that matter to the customer, not just to hit a quota. When you prioritize their success and tie your value to their goals, trust grows fast — and so does your influence.

Step 2 – Focus on Bringing Something of Value

Any time you work with a customer, and in every interaction, try to bring something of value. This is how you become someone worth making time for. Customers have choices, and their time is limited. If you want to be their choice, every minute they spend with you needs to feel worthwhile.

Value might come in the form of insights, introductions, or problem-solving. Or it could be more tangible, like bringing coffee to a morning meeting or helping a contact network within your company. Whatever the form, value is about impact, not flair, not flash, and definitely not fluff.

I used to think that taking a customer to a nice dinner or sporting event was the key to unlocking more opportunities. That is, until I met a customer who straight-up told me otherwise. We were sitting in great seats at a home game of his favorite professional sports team when he turned to me and asked, *"So, did you finish that proposal I asked for?"*

Unfortunately, I hadn't. And worse, I hadn't done everything I could to get it done. When I told him I'd need more time, the disappointment on his face said it all. Then he added, *"You know, I appreciate you taking me to the game tonight, but getting that proposal to me would have meant more."*

That moment stuck with me. I spent the rest of the game thinking not about the score, but about that conversation and how quickly I wanted to get back to the office and make things right.

It was a wake-up call. What I thought was valuable didn't align with what *he* valued. After that day, we went to a few more games together, but I always made sure he had every proposal, answer, or update *before* we met in person. And you know what? That led to far more wins than any ballgame ever did.

The takeaway is simple: know what your customer values, and make it your priority. Don't confuse entertainment for service. **What earns trust and deepens relationships isn't what you give, it's what you solve.**

Sometimes, yes, a round of golf or tickets to a big game *can* move the needle. But they should *never* come at the expense of delivering the real value your customer needs most.

Step 3 – Be Responsive When They Need You

Responsiveness demonstrates reliability, and reliability builds trust. When a customer reaches out, especially in a moment of need, your response becomes part of how they define the relationship.

It could be a late shipment. A technical question. An unexpected internal deadline. Regardless of the size of the issue, your speed, tone, and willingness to help in that moment matter more than the actual outcome.

Responding doesn't mean solving the issue on the spot. It simply means acknowledging the request, confirming you're on it, and following through. A quick reply that says, "Got it, I'm digging in now and will update you shortly," shows that you're present, engaged, and accountable.

Over time, your consistency in these small moments will position you as someone they can depend on. Not just when it's convenient, but every time.

Step 4 – Learn to Love What You Sell

You don't need to have a lifelong passion for your company's product, but you do need to find something about it that genuinely excites you. Why? Because enthusiasm is contagious, and customers can tell the difference between someone who's just selling a product and someone who actually believes in it.

Take the time to really learn what sets your product or service apart. Use it yourself if you can. Talk to colleagues about why they believe in it. Understand where it shines — and where it doesn't.

My favorite example of this comes from my time selling cleaning products. I'd never been much of a cleaner before, but once I started the job, I dove in headfirst. I tested every product and scrubbed every surface in my house.

One product stood out: a foaming spray designed for shower walls and bathtubs. It worked so well, I was genuinely blown away. From that point on, anytime I needed to talk up my brand, I defaulted to telling a story about using that product to clean an old, neglected basement tub. I didn't have to exaggerate or "sell," I just shared the story. Because I believed in what I was saying, I could focus entirely on the conversation and the relationship, not the pitch.

That's the goal. When you know and love your product, you talk about it differently. You talk like someone who wants to share something valuable, not someone checking boxes on a deck.

This doesn't mean pretending it's perfect. Credibility comes from honesty. If a customer raises a concern and they're right, acknowledge it. Then show them what your product does exceptionally well. Knowing your strengths and being transparent about your gaps builds credibility and gives your message staying power.

Once you find something you genuinely believe in about your product, you'll start talking about it more naturally and more persuasively. And when selling becomes second nature, it frees you up to focus on your customer instead of the sale.

Step 5 – Build Personal Connections

The fastest way to transform a contact into a partner is to find something real to connect over. That could be a shared hobby, a sports team, a hometown, or even a common perspective on how to run a meeting.

Finding common ground isn't about forcing small talk. It's about paying attention. Look at what's in their background during video calls. Listen to the analogies they use. Take note of what lights them up when they speak.

Let's say you're a golfer. If you notice a putting mat in a customer's office, don't just admire it silently; ask a question. "Are you a golfer?" If they say yes, boom — you've got a connection. From there, it becomes easier to build rapport, tell stories, and eventually, maybe even schedule time to hit the course together.

Connections give you a bridge. The more of those you have, the stronger the relationship becomes and the more likely the customer is to choose you when it matters most.

Step 6 – Do Your Job and Do it Well

The foundation of every strong relationship is competence. All the lunches and friendly conversations in the world won't matter if you don't deliver when the stakes are high.

Get the details right. Communicate clearly. Follow through. Make your customer's job easier. If something goes wrong, own it and fix it fast.

When customers know they can count on you to show up, solve problems, and get results, you earn the one thing every relationship needs most: trust.

And once you're trusted? Every recommendation you make will carry more weight because they know you've got their back.

Just the other day, I delivered a savings report to a new customer, one tied directly to a C-level goal. The findings were exciting: massive cost reductions, big wins on paper. There was only one problem: the data was wrong. It overstated the savings by nearly 50%.

I realized the error shortly after delivering the report, but it was too late to "unshare" the results. So I owned it. Fast.

I corrected the report, alerted the account owner, and offered to take full responsibility. Instead, they stepped up and took accountability themselves and asked if I'd walk the customer through the corrected version to rebuild confidence.

I did. And while the savings weren't quite what we'd hoped, they were still meaningful. More importantly, we earned trust by handling the mistake head-on. No deflection. No hiding. Just fast action, clear communication, and transparency.

That customer saw what we were made of. Not just in good times, but when things went wrong. That's when trust is really built.

Final Thought

None of these steps work in isolation. But together — practiced consistently — they create something powerful: trust. And trust is what turns transactions into partnerships.

Relationships aren't built in a day; they're built every day. Not through grand gestures, but through steady effort, honest communication, and showing up when it counts.

Do that, and your relationships won't just help you grow accounts; they'll open doors, earn you advocates, and outlast any product or pitch.

Chapter 10 Recap

Key Takeaways

- Long-term relationships are the key to success in account management. Sales follow trust.
- A strong relationship can turn a "maybe" into a "yes".
- Doing your job well is the most consistent way to earn and deepen trust.

Reflection Questions

- Think about your best customer relationship. How did it start, and how has it grown?
- How do you consistently add value between major touchpoints?

Apply It Now

- Identify one current customer where the relationship feels one-sided. What can you do to provide more value to your customer and make it mutually beneficial?
- Find a natural opportunity this week to connect with a customer on a shared interest, background, or goal, and see where the conversation takes you.

Chapter 11

Customer Obsession

Not long ago, I was in a meeting, pitching hard, not to a customer, but to my own leadership team. I was advocating for a major internal investment to support a joint initiative with one of my key accounts. It was a bold ask: more money, more resources, and no guaranteed return — just a promise of deeper access to their sales team and a shot at long-term growth.

After I wrapped up my case, my manager looked at me and asked, half-joking, half-concerned, *"Do you work for us or for them?"*

I've never received a better unintentional compliment.

The truth is, I *do* work for "us," but when I'm doing my job right, it can be hard to tell. I knew what that customer was trying to achieve, and I knew this investment would move the needle for them *and* for us. The lines were blurred, and that's exactly where great account managers live.

When you're truly customer-obsessed, you still represent your company, but you operate like and embedded partner inside your customer's world. Their goals become your goals. Their wins feel personal. Their setbacks keep you up at night.

That's not bias. That's how you earn trust. And that's how you drive growth.

To truly succeed as an account manager, you have to go beyond providing good service. You need to live and breathe your customer's goals, treating their success as inseparable from your own.

Nearly every salesperson claims to be "customer-focused." Most will say they put the customer's needs first. But in account management, that's just table stakes. True success demands more. It requires customer obsession — a mindset where you're not just aligned with the customer, you're all-in.

Customer obsession doesn't just mean listening; it means advocating. It pushes you past expectations into exceeding them. And while that level of service may occasionally conflict with internal quotas, timelines, or goals, it's the long game that wins in this role.

When you're consistently aligned with your customer's success, you become more than a vendor. You become a partner they can't imagine doing business without.

Let's take a closer look at what that really looks like and how you can build it into your approach, meeting by meeting.

– A Crash Course in Customer Obsession –

Customer obsession isn't one grand gesture; it's a series of small, intentional actions that prove you're in it for more than just the sale. The steps ahead will show you how to build that reputation, one decision at a time.

Step 1 – Walk in Your Customer's Shoes

To become customer-obsessed, you must see the world through your customer's eyes and walk in their shoes. This goes far beyond understanding product usage or delivery schedules. It means grasping the full chain of impact your role has on their business, from the frontline employees to the boardroom.

Let's say you sell bubble wrap and your customer's shipment is delayed. Sure, the surface-level issue is that they don't have protective packaging. But dig deeper: What happens next? They can't ship out fragile goods. Their own customer cancels an order. Their reputation suffers. The consequences ripple outward.

Maybe their operations manager, your main contact, is now answering questions from senior leadership about the delay. Maybe they're worried about losing their job if the issue happens again. Suddenly, you're not just fixing a logistics problem. You're preserving trust, protecting careers, and reinforcing your own value in the process.

Walking in your customer's shoes means understanding what they're up against, and then feeling that pressure as if it were your own. To do this:

- Ask smarter questions.
- Find out what your contact is accountable for,
- Understand how their performance is measured,
- Learn what success looks like from their perspective.

If your customer's goal is to increase margins by five percent and yours is to sell 1,000 units at full price, don't just push for the units. Fight for their margin. Your success follows theirs, not the other way around.

Step 2 – Be Your Customer's Champion

Being customer-obsessed isn't just about hearing what your customer needs; it's about owning it. That means consistently showing up as someone who represents, advocates, and fights for your customer, even when it's inconvenient. Great account managers are seen by their customers as an extension of their team. That starts by earning their trust and proving you'll use it well.

To champion your customer effectively, you have to internalize their goals as if they were your own. For example:

- If their top priority is launching a new product on time, make it yours, too.
- If they're measured on reducing waste, start thinking in terms of efficiency.
- If they're focused on expansion, be the one bringing new opportunities to the table.

That level of alignment changes the way you show up. Suddenly, you're not just delivering a service; you're delivering wins.

This doesn't mean being blindly loyal or forgetting your own responsibilities. It means taking what you know about your customer's needs and using your credibility internally to advocate for them. And when things go sideways, it means showing up when it's hardest.

I'm reminded of a time when I managed a customer who needed more time to fulfill an obligation. They had committed to a large inventory purchase during a period of extreme product scarcity, anticipating demand from one of their own customers. But that demand didn't come as expected. If they had followed through on our original agreement, they would have been significantly overstocked and faced serious financial risk.

I knew it would be tough, but I worked internally to secure a temporary exception for them to scale back. There was little appetite for it. It cost me sales, and leadership wasn't thrilled.

However, I knew that pushing forward would damage the relationship and possibly cost my primary contact her job. By buying her time and space, we preserved the partnership. She later found new buyers, fulfilled the full commitment on a slower timeline, and we continued working together for years afterward.

Situations like this reveal whether you're merely customer-focused or truly customer-obsessed. Anyone can support a customer when things are easy. Champions step up when things are hard.

And sometimes, championing your customer means taking their needs back to your company and making the case for why they matter. That's where internal selling comes in, and it deserves a strategy all its own.

Step 3 – Master the Art of Internal Selling

Customer obsession doesn't stop at understanding your customer's needs. You also need to effectively sell those needs within your own organization.

That's what internal selling is all about: helping your company care about your customer's priorities as much as you do and influencing your internal teams to take customer priorities seriously, even when they compete with other demands. And the better you get at it, the more likely your customer is to get what they actually need, not just what's easiest to provide.

It's easy to promise customers the world; it's much harder to secure real buy-in internally, especially when it involves limited resources, shifting timelines, or custom solutions.

This is where great account managers distinguish themselves. Not in what they say, but in what they can rally support for behind the scenes. Your ability to navigate this complexity is what transforms good service into an exceptional partnership. To do this well, you need to:

- **Know your company's priorities.** When you understand what your leadership values — margin, growth, brand visibility — you can frame your customer's needs in ways that resonate. Don't just say, "The customer needs this." Say, "If we meet this need, we'll unlock X revenue and position ourselves as a strategic partner."
- **Bring the right level of detail.** Come prepared with facts and clear, concise information that helps decision-

makers weigh the trade-offs. What's the ask? What's the timeline? What's the impact if we say yes or no?
- **Build internal relationships.** Your influence doesn't come from your title. It comes from trust. If the pricing, operations, or legal team sees you as credible and collaborative, they'll work with you, not around you.

I once had a customer who was poised to launch our product line across their retail stores, but only if we could deliver customized display materials on an accelerated timeline. It wasn't in the budget, and the marketing team had other priorities. Rather than accept a default "no," I pitched it internally as a strategic investment: we'd secure first-to-shelf advantage, increase velocity, and position ourselves for broader expansion. I showed them the math, the timeline, and the growth potential. That shift in framing earned approval. The display units were produced, the product was launched on schedule, and it became one of our best performers.

Internal selling isn't about getting everything you ask for. It's about showing your team that what you're asking for is worth doing. When they trust your judgment, they're more likely to follow your lead. And that's what your customer needs most from you: someone who can get things done.

> **Pro Tip: A Seat At the Table**
>
> If your customer were to listen in on your internal meeting, would they feel represented? They should.
>
> A truly customer-obsessed account manager speaks for their customer when they're not in the room — clearly, credibly, and with conviction. When your internal team knows you bring forward only the asks that matter, they'll listen. And when your customer knows you fight for what they need, they'll trust you to lead.

Step 4 – Own Your Role, Respect Theirs

Customer obsession isn't just about empathy; it's about execution. While Step 1 focused on understanding your customer's situation, this step is about what you do with that understanding.

Account management is a shared mission. Your customer has their job. You have yours. But your success depends on how well you support theirs.

That means taking full ownership of your responsibilities and delivering on them in a way that helps, not hinders, your customer's goals. You're not just a messenger. You're a problem solver, a fixer, a translator, and a catalyst. Your ability to simplify, follow through, and find workarounds is the reason your customer sticks with you.

And just as importantly, you need to stay mindful of the pressures your customer is under. If they're up against a deadline, don't add noise; bring clarity. If they're taking a risk by choosing you, do everything in your power to make that risk feel smart.

One time, I was trying to get a new product placed during a major retail reset. The catch? The customer needed physical resets across hundreds of stores, a project that was out of budget and logistically painful. I didn't punt it back to them; I stepped in. I split the cost, draining my own budget, and even handled resets myself in stores within driving distance. It was messy, manual, and way outside my job description, but it got the job done. And it sent a message: I'm not just here when it's easy. I'm here to make things work.

Your job doesn't exist in isolation. It exists because your customer needs someone like you to do it well. So do it well and do it in a way that makes their job easier.

Step 5 – Practice, Practice, Practice

Customer obsession isn't something you declare. It's something you prove, over and over, in the moments most people overlook.

It's a habit, one you build through repetition, reflection, and refinement.

It shows up in how you follow up. In how you handle ambiguity. In how you stay late to chase down answers or show up early to get ahead of problems. These moments don't always show up in reports, but they show up in relationships. And those are what matter most.

Being customer-obsessed means:

- Solving problems you didn't cause.
- Showing up when no one asked you to.
- Pushing for your customer's success even when there's nothing in it for you... yet.

But here's the thing: it always comes back around. Customers don't forget the people who made their lives easier, who made them look good, or who showed up when it counted.

Yes, it will cost you time and energy in the short term. But it will earn you trust, loyalty, and access to opportunities that others never even hear about.

Customer obsession is more than a mindset; it's a muscle. The more you use it, the stronger it gets. Over time, this commitment becomes your edge. Not every competitor will go as far, listen as closely, or care as deeply. That's your advantage. Build a reputation as the account manager who shows up when it matters, and you won't just earn business, you'll earn loyalty. And that lasts a lot longer than any single deal.

Final Thought

"Do you work for us or for them?" It was meant as a question, maybe even a critique. But the truth is, it was the clearest sign I was doing my job right. When you're customer-obsessed, the lines start to blur — and that's a good thing.

You still represent your company, but you operate with your customer's goals in mind and their success as your mission. That's not disloyalty. That's partnership. And in account management, it's the strongest foundation you can build.

Chapter 11 Recap

Key Takeaways

- Customer obsession is about knowing what keeps your customer up at night, then helping them sleep easier.
- You win more in the long term by making their goals your own, even when that creates short-term friction.
- Internal selling is just as important as external. Advocate with clarity and intention.

Reflection Questions

- Have you ever prioritized your goal over your customer's? How did it impact the outcome?
- When was the last time you sold your company on doing what's right for the customer?

Apply It Now

- Identify one customer goal you've been ignoring or under-prioritizing. What can you do this week to support it?
- Pick a recent customer "no" from your company. Could it be turned into a "yes" if you advocated harder internally?

Chapter 12

Presentation Building

A few years ago, I was preparing for a meeting with a new customer. I'd spent weeks trying to get on their calendar and finally managed to get some time with them. The only thing left was to present what I wanted to pitch.

I pulled together slides from past decks, threw in a few screenshots, and told myself it was "good enough." After all, I knew the story. I was confident I could fill in the gaps live.

But from the first slide, I could feel it: they weren't buying it. The message was unclear. The formatting was off.

I did my best to power through, trying to recover with my delivery, but the deck never gave me a chance. It wasn't tight. It wasn't tailored. It wasn't ready.

Needless to say, my pitch didn't land, and the customer did not buy what I was trying to sell. The product was right. The timing was right. But the presentation? It cost me the deal.

That's when I realized something most account managers learn the hard way: your deck isn't just a support tool. It's your first impression, your best shot, and often your silent salesperson. Done well, it builds clarity and confidence. Done poorly, it undermines both.

Every meeting is an opportunity to win or lose influence, and presentations are often the deciding factor.

Whether your meeting is virtual or in person, internal or external, chances are you'll need a presentation to support your pitch. The format might be anything from PowerPoint slides and printed handouts to whiteboards and demos, but the goal is the same: to deliver a message that informs, persuades, and sticks.

And here's the reality: most account managers are on their own. No design team. No ghostwriter. Just whatever templates or past decks they can scavenge. But that's okay.

You don't need a fancy presentation. You need one that works.

That means knowing how to build with purpose, using tools well, and tailoring your message to the audience. A well-built presentation doesn't guarantee a win, but a bad one can absolutely cost you the deal.

Let's walk through how to build better decks faster and make sure your next meeting works in your favor.

– A Crash Course in Building Great Presentations –

Great presentations don't happen by accident; they're built with intention. The following steps will help you sharpen your approach, whether you're building from scratch or leveling up an existing deck. Start with the basics, build toward clarity, and always keep your customer at the center.

Step 1 – Learn to use PowerPoint

If there's one skill that will pay immediate dividends, it's knowing how to build a PowerPoint presentation. You don't need to be an expert designer, but you do need to know how to create and format slides that are clean, legible, and clear.

At a minimum, that means:

- Avoid flashy animations and sound effects. You're not in middle school anymore.
- Stick to simple, professional fonts and layouts.
- Focus on clarity, not flair. Your slides are there to support your message, not compete with it.

Most importantly, invest the time to get comfortable with the tool. PowerPoint is the industry standard for a reason, learn the basics and build from there.

> **Pro Tip: Master a Tool, Not *Every* Tool**
>
> PowerPoint is the most widely used presentation software in business, and for good reason. But it's not your only option. Keynote, Google Slides, and other platforms can work just as well. The key isn't which one you use, it's how well you use it. Pick one, learn its strengths, and get fast. Great account managers don't waste time fumbling through formatting; they build with confidence in whatever tool they've mastered.

Step 2 – Move Beyond Novice Level

It's okay to start as a beginner. But if you want to get faster and build better decks, you'll need to improve your skills.

Why?

Because when you're better at building decks:

- You'll spend less time formatting and more time thinking.
- Your decks will look more polished and persuasive.
- You'll feel more confident presenting them.

If it takes you two hours to build a basic deck today, improving your skills could cut that time in half, freeing you up to focus on strategy, messaging, or prepping for customer questions.

And better decks lead to better meetings. Nobody wants to sit through a slide full of dense text. Use visuals, charts, and infographics to break up content and support your points.

You don't need to master every feature. But improving your working knowledge will make you faster, more confident, and more persuasive.

Step 3 – Be Resourceful

Being a great presenter doesn't mean creating everything from scratch. Start with:

- Templates from your marketing or sales enablement teams.
- Slides you've used in the past.
- Presentations shared by colleagues or managers.
- Internal repositories or decks from previous campaigns.

Even if your company doesn't have a formal deck library, you can build one yourself. Over time, you'll develop a collection of slides you can pull from and customize.

Every new deck should get easier. Save your best slides and reuse what works; your future self will thank you. However, be sure to double-check all references, especially customer names. A leftover name from a previous deck can derail trust.

And if you're not using PowerPoint? You'll need to get creative and use:

- Live product demos
- Printed handouts
- Short videos or interactive elements
- Physical samples (if appropriate for the setting)

Whatever you use, make sure it supports your message and fits the space and format of the meeting. Don't bring a bulky demo to a virtual meeting or assume your customer has audio set up to hear a video. Plan accordingly.

Step 4 – Focus on What You Want to Accomplish

This is one of the biggest mistakes account managers make: building slides without a clear goal.

Every presentation should be designed to drive toward a specific outcome. Ask yourself:

- What do I want my audience to do after this meeting?
- What message or idea do I want to leave them with?

Then reverse-engineer your deck to lead them there.

Don't clutter it with unnecessary product specs or backstory if that's not relevant. Instead, build a story arc that moves from problem to solution with your product, service, or recommendation as the bridge.

If a slide doesn't support your goal, cut it. If it's unclear what action you want the customer to take, clarify it.

> **Pro Tip: Build Backward from the Ask**
>
> Before you open a blank slide, write down the action you want your audience to take. That's your north star. Whether it's a yes, a follow-up, or a commitment, every slide should earn its place by moving your audience closer to that outcome. If it doesn't help you get to the ask, it doesn't belong in the deck.

Step 5 – Build for the Actual Time Slot and Venue

You can build a brilliant presentation and still fail if it's not designed for the meeting itself. Before you build, ask:

- How long is the meeting?
- Will it be in-person or virtual?

- Will I have access to a screen, projector, or sound system?
- How large is the audience?

Then adapt your content accordingly.

A 30-minute virtual meeting requires tight pacing and clear visuals. You may only have 20 minutes of real time to speak. Meanwhile, a 90-minute in-person meeting gives you more space for demos, dialogue, and storytelling.

Likewise, a large room requires big visuals. Don't show off a pocket-sized product to an audience in the back row. On the other hand, a small group around a conference table might benefit from tactile materials or handouts.

If you're presenting somewhere unfamiliar, ask in advance about the tech setup. If needed, bring your own projector, cables, or backup materials.

In-person meetings open the door to physical materials like samples, handouts, and displays, which can help make your message stick.

Step 6 – Give Yourself Enough Time and Block It Off

Preparation is your differentiator. If your meeting is worth taking, it's worth preparing for.

And that means blocking time to build your deck. Don't rely on last-minute cramming between calls or late-night gaps; it rarely works. A rushed deck is easy to spot... and hard to recover from. Instead of rushing at the last minute:

- Block time to prepare as soon as a meeting is scheduled.
- Give yourself a minimum of one hour for a short deck, more for longer sessions.
- Expect to revise it once or twice before finalizing.

Start early enough that you can revisit the deck with fresh eyes before the meeting. You'll often catch mistakes or opportunities you missed in the first pass.

Think back to the story at the start of this chapter. Had I carved out time to prepare, the outcome could've been completely different. Don't make the same mistake. Great presentations aren't rushed; they're built with intention. Block the time, do the work, and give your message the attention it deserves.

Building a great presentation isn't about being a design expert; it's about being clear, intentional, and prepared. The fundamentals help you build something solid. But once you've got the basics down, it's the small enhancements that take your deck from good to great.

With the core deck in place, it's time to level up. The following tips will help you sharpen the edges, focus your message, and make your presentation truly persuasive.

Enhancing Your Deck: Presentation Tips That Add Impact

Once your core presentation is in place, it's time to level up. Great account managers don't just deliver information; they deliver it with clarity, confidence, and impact. The following tips aren't about flash; they're about focus. Use them to sharpen your message, boost engagement, and make sure your deck sticks with your audience long after the meeting ends.

Tip 1 – Anchor Your Presentation Around a Core Message

Your audience should walk away remembering one clear takeaway.

- Start by asking yourself: "If they forget everything else, what's the one thing I want them to remember?"
- Frame that message in clear, benefit-focused language.
- Use your first slide to introduce the message and your last slide to reinforce it.

- Use headlines and callouts that repeat or support the core idea throughout.

A strong core message makes your presentation stick. Make it simple, repeat it often, and build everything around it.

Tip 2 – Use Visual Metaphors

Smart visuals do more than decorate; they deepen understanding and recall.

- Replace dense descriptions with imagery that conveys the same concept more intuitively.
- Match the metaphor to your audience. Use industry-relevant symbols or analogies.
- Don't overdo it. One or two metaphorical visuals can have more impact than a slide full of them.
- Pair the metaphor with your spoken narrative to help tie the concept to your message.

The right metaphor doesn't just explain, it connects. Use it to make your message memorable.

Tip 3 – Minimize Text, Maximize Spoken Value

Your slides support your message; they shouldn't compete with you for attention.

- Aim for no more than six words per line and six lines per slide.

- Use bolded keywords and concise bullet points instead of complete sentences.
- Think of your slides as visual signposts; your voice fills in the story.
- If it must be text-heavy (e.g., for technical specs), talk the audience through your slides. Don't read them.

Slides should support your voice, not compete with it. Keep them clean so your message comes through loud and clear.

Tip 4 – Design for Readability Across All Devices

What's clear on your screen might be unreadable on theirs.

- Use 24-30 point font for body text; 36 point or larger is ideal for headers.
- Stick to sans-serif fonts like Arial, Calibri, or Helvetica for clarity.
- Use spacing, shapes, or arrows to visually guide the audience through your logic.
- Avoid clutter and include only one main idea per slide.

If your audience can't read it, they won't remember it. Prioritize clarity every time.

Tip 5 – Include "Reset" Slides to Refocus Attention

In longer presentations, these give the audience a mental refresh and re-engage their attention.

- Use a full-screen image with a big quote or single stat to punctuate transitions.
- Insert a slide with a bold question to spark curiosity for what's next.
- Consider brief interactive moments (like a show-of-hands question) to create engagement.
- Reset slides should be visually distinct with different colors, fonts, or layouts from your core slides.

Attention fades fast. A well-timed reset slide can pull your audience back in and keep your message on track.

Tip 6 – Prepare for Tech Glitches

No matter how polished your deck is, technology can, and will, fail.

- Save a PDF version of your deck to avoid formatting surprises.
- Email yourself a backup copy and keep it in the cloud or on a USB drive.
- Test your setup ahead of time, especially when presenting in person or with new platforms.
- Be ready to deliver the key message without slides if necessary.

Glitches are inevitable. Preparation isn't just smart, it's part of delivering like a pro.

These tips aren't about adding polish for polish's sake; they're about increasing impact. When your deck is clear, focused, and easy to follow, your message lands stronger and sticks longer.

Presentations matter; make yours work as hard as you do.

Final Thought

A good presentation won't win a deal on its own, but a bad one can absolutely lose it. Customers aren't just evaluating your product; they're evaluating how clearly you understand their needs and how effectively you can communicate your value. That's what your presentation is there to prove.

So don't wing it. Build with purpose. Prepare with care. Whether it's five slides or fifty, virtual or in-person, every presentation is a chance to earn trust, drive momentum, and move the conversation forward.

When your slides are clear and your message is sharp, you won't just present, you'll persuade.

Chapter 12 Recap

Key Takeaways

- Strong presentations are strategic, not decorative. They should drive toward a decision or outcome.
- Templates save time, but personalization builds credibility.
- Simplify your slides. Too much content is worse than too little.
- Decks don't build themselves; schedule the time before it slips away.

Reflection Questions

- Is your deck designed for the customer or for you?
- Do your slides support your message, or distract from it?

Apply It Now

- Revisit a recent deck and ask yourself: What can I remove, replace, or clarify?
- Schedule time on your calendar now for your next big presentation... and use it.

Chapter 13

Presenting, Pitching, and Selling

Earlier this year, I gave a presentation to a room full of top buyers from several major customers. I walked them through tools and features on our site, highlighting how they could streamline purchasing and drive value across their organizations. It was one of those meetings where everything just clicked. The message landed, the engagement was high, and by the end, the room was buzzing with follow-up questions.

Afterward, one of the buyers pulled me aside and said, *"That was one of the best presentations I've ever sat through. Not only am I sold on what you were showing us, I need to know, what's your secret to presenting so well?"*

The compliment was appreciated, but the real takeaway wasn't style; it was substance. The presentation worked because it was clear, customer-relevant, and purposefully structured. It didn't just inform, it persuaded. That's the goal of every great presentation: to move your audience toward action.

Every meeting is an opportunity. Your presentation sets the stage, your pitch delivers the value, and your success is measured by the progress you create — whether that's a decision, a next step, or a closed deal. And in account management, you're always selling something, even if it's just trust.

The best account managers understand that presenting, pitching, and selling aren't separate skills, they're interconnected. Unlike traditional sales reps who often focus on short-term transactions, account managers sell with the long game in mind. They pitch solutions, not just products. They use every presentation to build clarity, strengthen relationships, and create momentum.

Because even when the deal doesn't close that day, the right presentation plants the seed and positions you as the partner who can help it grow.

– A Crash Course in Delivering a Great Presentation –

Delivering a great presentation isn't just about having strong slides; it's about how you bring them to life. What you say, how you say it, and how you respond in the moment all influence how your message lands. The steps that follow will help you present with purpose, pitch with clarity, and sell with confidence.

Step 1 – Prepare Your Presentation and Talk Track

Start with your presentation materials, but don't stop there. You also need a talk track, a plan for what you'll say and how you'll say it. Think of your deck as a visual roadmap, not a script. It should support your message, not replace your voice.

- Develop your slides around the core message you want to convey.
- Plan your transitions, pauses, and questions in advance.
- Take notes on what you'll emphasize on each slide.
- Anticipate common objections and prepare responses.

Your slides guide the room, but your talk track is what brings the message to life. Real persuasion comes from your voice, your pacing, and the confidence behind your words.

Step 2 – Practice Your Delivery

A well-built presentation means nothing without preparation. Practicing your delivery helps you refine your flow, sharpen your message, and gain confidence.

- Practice the introduction, core slides, and closing separately before putting them all together.

- Run full mock presentations to assess the timing and clarity of your content.
- Identify content that feels clunky or disconnected, and adjust as needed.
- Consider recording yourself or presenting to a colleague for feedback.

Even a small amount of practice can dramatically improve how confidently and effectively you deliver.

Step 3 - Deliver With Confidence

Your tone, presence, and energy will shape how your message is received. Even if your slides are perfect, poor delivery can kill the pitch.

- Use clear, confident language: no jargon, no filler, no profanity.
- Project your voice and vary your tone to emphasize key points.
- If you lose your place, pause calmly, regroup, and move forward.
- Keep your body language open and engaging, whether in person or on camera.

Confidence isn't about perfection; it's about presence. Show up ready, steady, and focused on helping the customer win.

Step 4 – Be Ready to Pivot

Even the best-prepared presentations can be thrown off course the moment a meeting starts. A surprise attendee, a shortened time slot, or technical issues can all force you to adjust your plan on the fly. Great account managers don't panic when this happens; they pivot with purpose. To pivot effectively:

- **Stay anchored to your core objective.** Ask yourself: What am I here to accomplish? What absolutely needs to be conveyed for the meeting to succeed?
- **Quickly reassess your plan.** Decide which slides or talking points are essential and which can be skipped or shortened.
- **Adjust for the audience.** If a senior stakeholder joins, your tone, content, and level of detail may need to shift.
- **Set expectations with confidence.** Acknowledge the change proactively: "Since we're adjusting on the fly, I'll focus on the key takeaways to respect everyone's time. Does that sound good?"
- **Lead with flexibility, not fluster.** Your ability to adapt signals confidence and professionalism. When done well, a pivot doesn't feel like a scramble; it feels like you're in control.

I once arrived for what I thought would be a casual, end-of-year review with a long-time contact. Moments before we began, he informed me that his VP would be joining. Suddenly, the meeting shifted from informal to formal, with an executive in a suit and a much more serious tone.

I had prepped a casual, relationship-focused deck. But I quickly pivoted. I leaned into the data-heavy supporting slides: investment stats, category growth, long-term strategy. I cut the anecdotes, tightened my language, and presented with executive-level focus.

The VP left impressed, and the conversation progressed with only minor additional support required. That pivot, executed in real-time, helped strengthen the relationship and the outcome.

A well-executed pivot doesn't just save the meeting; it elevates it.

Step 5 – Make It a Conversation

A presentation isn't a monologue. It's a chance to engage, not just inform.

- Ask questions throughout the presentation to draw people in.
- Use phrases like: "How does this compare to what you're currently doing?" or "Would this approach solve the issue we discussed last week?"
- Encourage participation, even informally, to maintain energy.

- If you lose your place, ask for help. Use a phrase like: "What were we just discussing again?" This humanizes you and invites connection.

People engage with people, not slides. Treat your audience like collaborators, not spectators.

Pro Tip: The Audience Will Bail You Out

Losing your train of thought mid-presentation can feel like a disaster, especially when all eyes are on you. But here's a secret: your audience is usually on your side. If you blank, don't panic. Take a breath, smile, and say something like, "I just lost my place. What were we just talking about?" Nine times out of ten, someone will jump in to help. Not only does it get you back on track, it also humanizes you and invites connection. People don't expect perfection; they respond to presence, poise, and how you handle the unexpected.

Step 6 – Show Up Ready

Your preparation doesn't end with your slides. When it's time to present, your energy, timing, and mindset matter.

- Arrive early. Technical hiccups or delays happen all the time.
- Make sure you're rested, fed, and focused. Don't present hungry or foggy.
- Have backups of your deck saved as a PDF, emailed to yourself, and stored online.
- If you're sharing video or audio, test it in advance.

The best presenters don't just show up; they arrive prepared, focused, and ready to make the moment count. That's what leaves a lasting impression.

You've set the stage with a strong presentation. Now it's time to land the message. A great pitch doesn't just inform, it inspires action. Let's break down how to make that happen.

– A Crash Course in Making a Great Pitch That Drives Sales –

Before you deliver a strong pitch, you need to build one, and that takes more than just a good idea and a few solid slides. It takes clarity, intention, and a deep understanding of what your customer actually needs. The following keys will help you craft a pitch that doesn't just sell a product, but builds belief, earns trust, and drives momentum.

Key 1 - Start With Impact

An account manager doesn't just pitch a product; they pitch impact. And that impact must be rooted in trust. Before building your pitch, ground yourself in your primary goal: strengthening the long-term relationship. Sales will come, but only when the customer believes your intent is aligned with their success.

To do that, start by answering three critical questions:

- What pain does this solve for your customer?
- What goal does it help them reach?
- Why is this the right time to act?

If you can't answer these for yourself, you're not ready to make a pitch.

Key 2 - Sell With Narrative, Not Pressure

The best pitches don't feel like pitches at all. They feel like a story the customer is discovering with you, one that ends with a clear solution that makes sense for their business.

The goal isn't to convince; it's to connect the dots. When the story is told well, the customer often reaches the conclusion before you even get to your final slide. To get there:

- Start with the customer's world. Their goals, their challenges, their language, not your features.
- Use narrative tools like data, analogies, or quick anecdotes to make your point stick.
- Let your solution emerge as the natural conclusion, not a bold ask.

I once had a customer tell me, *"You made it feel like I came up with the idea myself."* That's the sign of a pitch that's built on connection, not coercion.

But here's where a lot of account managers trip up: they try to create urgency by focusing too heavily on what could go wrong. I made that mistake once by opening a pitch with a warning that employees might make unauthorized purchases through a competitor's platform. Instead of creating urgency, it created suspicion: *"What can employees buy from your platform that they shouldn't?"* Suddenly, I was defending our compliance systems instead of pitching value.

The takeaway? Don't let your story backfire. Use it to clarify, not complicate. If you introduce risk, be sure it won't boomerang back on you. A great story builds trust. It helps the customer envision a better outcome and makes the decision feel like progress, not pressure. That's how strong relationships (and sales) are built.

Key 3 - Don't Wait to Pitch

A great pitch doesn't belong on just one slide; it should be felt throughout the presentation.

Too many account managers build toward a "big reveal" at the end, only to lose their audience along the way. Instead, weave your value proposition into the entire conversation so that by the time you reach the final recommendation, the customer already sees it coming — and wants it.

This isn't about being repetitive. It's about *reinforcement*.

- Introduce your core value early.
- Tie each section of your presentation back to that value.
- Reinforce benefits as they naturally arise in the conversation.
- Let the final "ask" feel like the most logical next step, not a surprise twist.
- Your customer should anticipate the pitch before you make it. That's how you know your story is working.

If Key 2 is about telling the story right, Key 3 is about *structuring* it right. Pacing, repetition, and alignment make sure your message sticks and that the pitch feels earned, not forced.

Key 4 – Sell Softly, But Clearly

As an account manager, your relationship with your customer is your most valuable asset. Don't jeopardize it by hard selling.

- Lead with insight, not pressure.
- Offer recommendations, not ultimatums.
- Let your customer feel they are choosing, not being pushed.

Sometimes, that means walking away from a pitch for now. I once recommended a new program to a long-time customer that would've helped them scale and save. I believed in it. But they weren't ready. Budgets were tight, leadership was changing, and the timing just didn't work.

Instead of pushing, I said, "No problem. When the time's right, I'll help you move fast." Three months later, I got the call: *"We're ready. Can you walk leadership through it again?"*

Because I didn't press, I was able to preserve the relationship. Because I stayed ready, I won the deal. Soft selling isn't about lowering the stakes; it's about earning the right to be at the table when the stakes are highest.

The best pitches don't rely on pressure; they rely on preparation, clarity, and connection. By approaching every pitch with intent and empathy, you position yourself as a partner, not just a seller.

Now that you know how to build and deliver a strong pitch, it's time to focus on the outcome: guiding your customer toward a confident, shared next step.

Final Thought

Whether you're pitching a product, a new idea, or your continued value as a partner, how you show up matters. A great pitch isn't just well-built, it's well-delivered, well-received, and rooted in what your customer cares about most.

Great pitches don't shout, they resonate. When you prepare thoughtfully, tell a clear story, and respect the customer's decision-making process, you earn more than attention; you earn trust.

Remember, a pitch isn't a performance. It's a conversation with purpose. Focus less on closing the deal and more on opening the door to long-term success. That's how relationships grow and how opportunities follow.

Now, let's explore what comes next: follow-up and follow-through, and the moments that turn a pitch into a win.

Chapter 13 Recap

Key Takeaways

- Every presentation is a pitch, whether you're selling an idea or a product.
- A strong pitch is customer-centered, solution-focused, and seamlessly integrated into your story.
- Relationship-based selling wins more often and more sustainably than high-pressure tactics.

Reflection Questions

- What's the real value your presentation delivers to the customer?
- Do your pitches strengthen or strain your customer relationships?

Apply It Now

- Build a pitch that focuses entirely on your customer's needs, not your own desired outcome.
- Present your deck to a colleague who doesn't know the context and ask them: What do you think I was trying to accomplish? Then compare their answer to your original intent.

Chapter 14

Follow-Up and Follow-Through

A while back, I pitched a bundled program to a customer that would consolidate their purchases, reduce costs, and give them stronger control. They liked it in theory but didn't commit right away. There were too many moving parts and too many stakeholders. After the meeting, I followed up with a clear summary, a few open questions, and a proposal to walk through it again with their broader team. I stayed patient, persistent, and kept the momentum alive.

Two weeks later, they agreed to a phased rollout.

But the real work started after the ink dried. I stayed involved through every implementation call, chased down internal approvals, and provided training to users who would be impacted by the change. It wasn't glamorous, but it got the job done.

A month later, everything was live. Three months in, they were outperforming forecast. Six months later, they came back asking what else we could help them streamline.

That deal didn't close because I pitched it perfectly. It closed and grew because I didn't disappear after the meeting. I stayed connected, first by following up until the deal was won, then by following through until it was successfully executed.

One opens the conversation. The other opens the relationship.

A "yes" is just the beginning. And even without one, what happens next determines your momentum.

Whether you've pitched a new initiative, made a sale, or left a meeting without a clear decision, what follows is critical. Many people think of selling as the final step. For account managers, it's only the midpoint. Follow-up earns attention and keeps opportunities alive. Follow-through earns belief. It's where execution becomes your edge and where promises turn into proof.

Account management is about long-term, trust-driven relationships. That means sticking around after the handshake. While a one-time salesperson might move on once a deal is done, you stay in the trenches — solving problems, mobilizing teams, chasing details, and driving outcomes.

Whether you're waiting on a decision or finalizing the details after one, your ability to follow up and follow through is what sets you apart and earns the next opportunity. Let's walk through how to do both well.

– A Crash Course in Great Follow-Up –

Follow-up isn't about checking a box; it's about moving conversations forward without breaking trust. The way you follow up signals your awareness, your intent, and your professionalism. Do it poorly, and you'll come across as pushy or impatient. Do it well, and you'll earn responses, build credibility, and keep opportunities alive. Here's how to follow up the right way.

Key 1 – Master Your Cadence

Follow-up is about timing as much as it is about content. Push too often, and you'll push your customer away. Wait too long, and opportunities die on the vine.

- Limit follow-ups to once per week for non-urgent needs.
- For time-sensitive or high-priority items, you can follow up more frequently, but only if it's truly justified.
- Use calendar reminders to ensure consistency without overdoing it.

- Remember: Being persistent is okay, being annoying is not. Your goal is to stay top of mind without becoming a nuisance.

When you respect timing, your follow-up feels thoughtful, not transactional.

> **Pro Tip: Don't Set It and Forget It**
>
> Calendar reminders are helpful, but cadence isn't one-size-fits-all. What feels timely to one customer might feel pushy to another. Before every follow-up, ask yourself: *Has anything changed that makes this message more or less welcome today?* A smart cadence adapts. The goal isn't to follow up on schedule; it's to follow up when it's helpful.

Key 2 – Make Every Follow-Up a Give and Take

Following up should feel helpful, not annoying. Keep the conversation alive by adding value, not repeating old requests.

- Skip "Just checking in." Bring something new: an update, data, or a new idea.
- Use fresh touchpoints to maintain contact and gather context passively.

- Don't chase a "yes" so aggressively that your customer stops responding altogether.
- Offer value to earn attention.

Not long ago, I was waiting for a customer's reply about moving some large quantity purchasing to my platform. I'd followed up twice, once a week, as usual. The first message received a polite response of, "We need more time," but the second went unanswered. I knew another nudge without new value wouldn't help and might push them away.

I also knew they'd been trying unsuccessfully to get an answer on something outside my area from another division. So, I dug into our internal contacts, found someone in the right department, and after a few tries, got a response. I arranged for them to connect with my customer.

Then, I followed up again, not just asking for an update on my proposal, but also mentioning: "By the way, I spoke with Joe from division XY yesterday and he's open to connecting with you about your question. Let me know when it would be a good time for that conversation."

That message earned a reply. Not a "yes" to moving forward with the purchasing shift, but context, clarity, and a timeline. Which was more progress than I'd made in weeks.

The takeaway? When your follow-up offers value — insight, help, or connections — you open the door to better responses.

Key 3 – Approach Every Follow-Up with Empathy

Your follow-up is a reflection of your awareness, not just of your own needs, but of your customer's reality.

- Always remember that your customer is a human being, not just a professional contact.
- Life, workload, and internal politics all affect timing.
- Leading with empathy helps maintain trust, even when answers are slow.
- Aggressive or impatient follow-up can damage long-term relationships, no matter the intent.

One of my biggest lessons came when a customer I thought was excited suddenly ghosted me after a pitch. I followed up multiple times with no reply, then broke my own rules by sending a long, emotional message pleading for a response. Not my finest moment.

Eventually, I got a reply. It was short and to the point, but not at all what I had expected: *"Sorry Bill, my dad passed away last weekend and I haven't made it back to the office yet. I promise I'll get back to you early next week. I just need a little time."*

I felt like a complete idiot.

I was so focused on the pitch that I missed the person. That moment reminded me: empathy isn't just kindness, it's situational awareness. I'd forgotten my customer was a person with a life far more important than my proposal. I apologized and timed a small gesture to their return. The relationship survived, but that won't always be the case.

This experience taught me: never assume silence means indifference. You never know what's going on behind the scenes. Be gracious, thoughtful, and human. Show genuine care instead of pressure, and your customer will remember when they're ready to reconnect.

Empathy isn't a tactic. It's your most reliable loyalty engine.

Key 4 – Be Patient, But Proactive

Patience is a competitive advantage. Customers don't operate on your schedule, and that's okay.

- Resist the urge to press too hard when you're waiting on a decision.
- Use the time to plan your next move or prepare additional materials.
- Demonstrate that you're steady, not desperate. This builds trust.
- When the answer finally comes, your calm professionalism will be remembered.

Patience earns trust, but preparation makes you ready when the moment comes.

Key 5 – Tell the Truth, Every Time

Honesty builds trust. Once lost, it's nearly impossible to regain.

- Never fabricate urgency or create false scarcity to force a decision.
- If timing truly matters, be transparent about why and what's at stake.
- If something has changed since your last meeting, update your customer quickly.
- Trust is your strongest currency. Protect it, even when it costs you a deal.

Your customer may forget details, but they won't forget if you came through.

You've kept the opportunity alive with smart, well-timed follow-up. Now it's time to deliver. Follow-through turns promises into proof and earns you the trust to take the next step.

– A Crash Course in Great Follow-Through –

Follow-through is where promises become proof. It's not the flashy part of the job, but it's the part your customer will remember. This is where reliability is built, trust is tested, and reputations are made. Let's break down what it takes to deliver after the "yes."

Key 1 – Prepare Before You Pitch

Follow-through starts *before* your customer says yes.

- Confirm product availability and the feasibility of execution in advance.
- Coordinate internally to ensure alignment across supply, delivery, and support.
- Avoid pitching what you can't deliver. It will cost you more than just a sale.
- Set realistic expectations up front, and you'll earn more trust on the back end.

A pitch backed by preparation builds confidence on both sides and sets the tone for everything that follows.

Key 2 – Do Whatever It Takes to Deliver

A great account manager will do whatever it takes to ensure their customers get what they need, even when it's messy, inconvenient, or wildly outside their formal job description.

- Follow-through isn't passive. It requires initiative, urgency, and a willingness to push through obstacles.
- Sometimes that means helping physically. Other times, it's about navigating internal roadblocks, coordinating

- logistics, or solving problems no one else wants to touch.
- Customers remember when you step up, and they remember when you don't.

A great example of this was a time when I sold a customer on adding a new item to their assortment. At the time of the pitch, the item was in stock and ready to ship. However, by the time their reset was scheduled and they were ready to bring it in, inventory had run dry due to a spike in demand. Suddenly, the item I had confidently pitched was no longer available, and my customer was expecting enough of it to execute a launch across all their locations.

I had two choices: disappoint my customer or fight to get them what they needed. I chose the latter. I quickly built a case for why this customer deserved priority access and outlined the long-term risk of falling short. Then I reached out to internal stakeholders, including other account managers, and persuaded them to shift volume to support the bigger opportunity.

In the end, I secured enough inventory, but it was scattered. I coordinated transfers from multiple locations, navigating emails and escalations to consolidate shipments and deliver on time.

When I called my customer with the good news, I could hear the relief and appreciation in their voice. That call solidified the relationship and reinforced their trust in me. Not just as someone who could pitch a great idea, but as someone who could deliver when it counted.

That's the heart of follow-through: owning the outcome, not just the idea, even when it's hard, inconvenient, or thankless. It's not about passing the baton; it's about proving to your customer that you'll go to bat for them every time.

Key 3 - Be An Internal Seller, Not a Squeaky Wheel

Sometimes, the only way to follow through on what you've sold is by influencing your internal organization as skillfully as you influence your customer.

- **Internal systems don't move themselves.** Other teams may not understand your customer's priorities or sense their urgency.
- **Build a strong case.** Tailor your ask to highlight revenue, reputation, or strategy.
- **Escalate wisely.** It's about focus, not blame, to prevent missed deadlines or lost chances.
- **Bridge the silos.** Own the problem, coordinate teams, and speak each stakeholder's language.
- **Push with purpose, not ego.** Be respectful, show thanks, and keep internal allies willing to help.

Remember: every internal win makes you a more reliable partner externally. If your customer trusts you, it's often because your team trusts you, too.

Think back to the earlier story: when inventory ran dry and logistics hit a wall, persistence wasn't enough. It took navigating politics, rallying support, and showing others why the customer's success mattered to them, too.

And if polite nudging isn't working, don't be afraid to escalate. Just make sure you've tried the right channels first and given your teammates fair notice.

That's the essence of internal selling: not just making noise, but making the right case, in the right way, to move the right people. That's how great account managers drive results behind the scenes.

Key 4 – Communicate, But Don't Create Panic

You don't have to share every hiccup, just the ones that matter.

- Give updates when there's news to share, especially if it's positive.
- If something might go wrong, assess first: is it real or just noise?
- Don't create unnecessary stress. Shield your customers from turbulence whenever possible.

- Communicate clearly, calmly, and proactively when real issues arise.

Thoughtful communication means sharing the right things at the right time.

> **Pro Tip: Don't Pull the Fire Alarm Too Early**
>
> It's tempting to flag every possible issue early, but premature panic is counterproductive. If you see a risk developing, don't immediately loop in your customer; own the problem first. Rally your internal team, explore fixes, and exhaust every option to avoid disruption. Only bring your customer in when there's a real, confirmed impact. Just be sure to do so while there's still enough time to get ahead of it together. Over-communicating worst-case scenarios too soon can cost you trust, credibility, and even future sales. Communicate proactively, not reactively, and always with purpose.

Key 5 – Match Your Promises with Performance

The easiest way to win long-term trust? Just do what you said you'd do.

- Avoid overpromising in the first place; only pitch what you can actually deliver.
- If circumstances change, update your customer honestly and do so in a timely manner.
- Great follow-through isn't flashy. It's consistent, dependable, and complete.
- Where possible, under-promise and over-deliver.

But be careful not to over-deliver in the wrong ways.

Going above and beyond can win trust, but only when the cost makes sense. I once saw a teammate volunteer our national account team to physically pick up unsold inventory from a customer's warehouses. It solved the customer's problem instantly, but we absorbed significant time, risk, and cost. In trying to be the hero, we created a quiet mess no one wanted to deal with. The pallets sat in garages and offices for over a year before we quietly paid to have them destroyed.

It taught me this: sometimes, doing "whatever it takes" can create new problems instead of solving old ones. Remember, boundaries matter.

Great follow-through isn't about heroics; it's about consistency, ownership, and doing what you said you would. When you deliver reliably and navigate challenges with professionalism, you don't just complete the work; you strengthen the relationship. That's how you turn a single win into lasting trust.

Final Thought

Great account managers don't win trust in the meeting; they earn it in the messy middle. Following up and following through aren't just professional courtesies; they're how you prove you'll deliver, even when no one's watching.

Follow-up is how you knock on the door. Follow-through earns you the key.

Master both, and you won't just win deals, you'll build partnerships that last.

Chapter 14 Recap

Key Takeaways

- Follow-up keeps opportunities alive. Follow-through earns long-term trust.
- Your work starts after the "yes." That's where deals succeed or fall apart.
- Protect your credibility by doing what you say, every time.
- Trust isn't built in the pitch, it's built in what happens next.

Reflection Questions

- Are you giving your customers enough space to make decisions, or pushing too hard?
- Do your follow-through habits build trust, or create extra stress?
- How well do you coordinate internally to ensure your promises become reality?

Apply It Now

- Send one follow-up message this week that adds value, not pressure.
- Look at an existing sale in flight. What can you do right now to ensure follow-through happens smoothly?

Chapter 15

Flexibility and Creativity

I once watched a teammate close a major deal using a product we technically didn't offer, at least not yet. The customer had a need that didn't line up with what we had on the shelf, and most people would've responded with, "We can't do that." But instead, he said, *"Let me see what's possible,"* and then worked across teams to build a solution from scratch.

It wasn't about bending the truth. It was about staying flexible, thinking creatively, and solving the problem without sticking to the script. That mindset didn't just win the deal; it built trust and opened the door to more business. And it all started with one simple choice: staying open, instead of shutting it down.

That's the kind of thinking great account managers bring to the table. Plans change. Customers ask for things that don't exist yet. Challenges pop up that aren't in the playbook. When those moments arrive — and they always do — your ability to adapt and innovate is what sets you apart.

Flexibility keeps you effective when things don't go as expected. Creativity helps you respond with solutions that surprise and deliver. Together, they help you navigate change, earn trust, and keep momentum when the path ahead is unclear.

Account management is a generalist role at its core. You don't need to be a technical expert in a specific industry to thrive; you need to be adaptable and solution-oriented. I started my career calling on people who sold annuities and life insurance, with no prior experience in either field. A friend of mine transitioned into ed-tech sales after working in school administration. He went from being the buyer to being the seller. Neither of us had all the answers at first, but we listened, learned, and thought differently to earn trust.

Flexibility and creativity aren't optional in this role. They're what help you navigate change, earn trust, and find a way forward when nothing is going according to plan.

– A Crash Course in Being Flexible –

Flexibility sounds like a soft skill, but in account management, it's a competitive edge. It's what helps you respond when plans change, customers surprise you, or your original approach just isn't landing. The following keys will help you build a flexible mindset, one that keeps you adaptable, collaborative, and ready for whatever comes next.

Key 1 – Put Your Pride on the Shelf

Flexibility starts with humility. That means being open to learning, even when you think you already know the answer.

- Ask questions without hesitation.
- Let others challenge your assumptions.
- Recognize that ego closes doors, but humility opens them.

You don't have to have all the answers. The best account managers ask good questions and stay curious. Admit what you don't know and learn from those around you, teammates, support staff, and even your customers.

A customer once told me, *"I don't care if you get it right the first time. I care that you adapt when it doesn't work."* That stuck with me. It reminded me that customers don't expect perfection, but they do expect responsiveness and growth.

You don't have to know everything. You just have to be teachable. That's what earns trust and keeps it.

Key 2 - Be Open to Ideas

Sometimes, the best path forward isn't your own. True flexibility means entertaining other people's approaches, even when they differ from your instincts. Being open to ideas requires curiosity and a collaborative mindset. These qualities not only support adaptability but also ignite creativity by expanding your perspective.

- Ask yourself: What if they're right?
- Replace defensiveness with curiosity.
- Dive into their reasoning. Seek to understand, not to critique.

This doesn't mean you stop thinking critically. It means you allow space for others to influence your thinking, including customers, teammates, and even competitors. In doing so, you broaden your toolkit and demonstrate real adaptability, setting the stage for creative solutions.

Key 3 - Be Willing to Try Something Different

Flexibility means being ready to pivot, even when that means leaving your original plan behind. This willingness to change course often requires extra effort and an openness to explore new paths, qualities that creativity will build upon.

- Evaluate what's working and what's not.
- Be honest with yourself when a plan needs to change.

- Don't cling to "your way" just because it was your idea.

A flexible account manager can switch gears quickly and intelligently. When something isn't landing with your customer, don't double down. Change it. Adjust it. Find a better route.

> **Pro Tip: Don't Marry the Plan**
>
> It's easy to fall in love with your own idea, especially when you've put in the work to build it. But sometimes, the best move is walking away from the plan you created. Your customer doesn't care how clever your strategy was; they care whether it works for them. If the plan's not landing, don't take it personally. Take it as a cue to pivot. Loyalty to outcomes beats loyalty to ego every time.

Key 4 – Practice, Practice, Practice

Flexibility sounds simple. Just be open, adaptable, and willing to change course. But in practice, it's one of the hardest things to do. That's why the best way to build it is through repetition.

- Use daily life as your training ground for flexibility.
- Take someone else's idea over your own, even when it's hard.

- Look for chances to give up control, even in small moments.

Being flexible can be deceptively difficult. I'm the first to admit that I struggle with it, both at work and at home. If this book hasn't already made it obvious, I have strong opinions about the "right" way to do things. And while I *know* I'm not always right, remembering that in the moment isn't always easy.

Letting my kids or wife choose the restaurant on a road trip has led to some surprisingly great meals, ones I never would've picked myself.

Letting a coworker shape the messaging strategy for a product launch resulted in better outcomes than my original plan.

In both cases, I had to give up control. And it paid off.

Reframing these moments as "reps" for being a better account manager has helped me embrace them. Instead of seeing them as giving in, I now view them as opportunities to build a more flexible mindset, one that makes me stronger when it really counts.

Every time you let someone else take the lead, you're strengthening your ability to adapt and respond. That's what flexibility is all about: letting go of control when it serves a better outcome.

Flexibility helps you adjust to what's happening. Creativity helps you imagine what's possible. Let's look at how to bring that second skill into play.

– A Crash Course in Being Creative –

Creativity isn't reserved for designers or inventors. It's a core account management skill. Whether you're solving a customer's problem, tailoring a pitch, or navigating a roadblock, creativity helps you see possibilities others miss. It's not about being showy. It's about thinking differently, trying new approaches, and finding practical solutions that work.

Let's break down how to bring creativity into your day-to-day work even when the path forward isn't obvious.

Key 1 – Think Outside the Box

Creativity starts with breaking free from routine. When you stretch beyond the obvious, you'll uncover fresh ways to solve problems and deliver value.

Cliché or not, this is the hallmark of a creative account manager. When a customer brings you a problem, chances are they've already tried the obvious solutions.

- Look at the issue from multiple angles.
- Consider what *could* be possible, even if it's not standard.
- Ask: "What would solve this, regardless of whether we've done it before?"

Once you've envisioned a solution, start reverse engineering it. Can your company do this? Can *you* make it happen? Many breakthroughs start as "unusual" ideas that someone was bold enough to pursue.

Key 2 – Draw From Past Experience

Creativity doesn't always mean inventing something new. More often, it's about repurposing something familiar in a fresh way.

- Think back to past campaigns, promotions, or messaging that worked.
- Repurpose those ideas to fit your current audience, product, or industry.
- Don't dismiss "old" ideas. Many of the best solutions are updated versions of something familiar.

Creativity isn't always flashy. Sometimes, being creative means recognizing an idea's essence, *what made it work*, and reimagining it to fit a new audience or moment.

When you're stuck, don't start from scratch. Dig into what you've seen, done, or borrowed in the past. Often, the best ideas are just smart updates of something that already worked.

> **Pro Tip: Put a New Twist on an Old Idea**
>
> Years ago, companies used to hand out branded matchbooks. They were cheap, practical, and widely used. You'd see a company's logo every time someone lit a cigarette or candle. It was visibility through usefulness.
>
> That approach obviously doesn't work today. Smoking is less common, and most brands don't want the association. But the core principle still holds: Give away something small, practical, and highly visible.
>
> Today's version? **Branded portable phone chargers**. Everyone has a smartphone, and keeping it charged is a universal challenge. A small power bank with your logo on it? That's something people will use daily. And every use keeps your brand front and center.

Key 3 - Ask Others for Help

Creative thinking doesn't happen in a vacuum. When you invite others into the problem-solving process, their ideas can spark breakthroughs you wouldn't reach alone.

Account managers face unique challenges that sometimes require ideas or resources beyond their immediate knowledge. While flexibility means being willing to ask for help when you need it, creativity thrives when you actively collaborate to explore new ideas and possibilities.

- Don't assume you have to figure everything out on your own.
- Leverage your teammates, your manager, and cross-functional partners who may have ideas or resources you haven't considered.
- Recognize that collaboration can be the spark your creativity needs.

Asking for help can be tough, but it can also be one of the easiest ways to give yourself a leg up. I remember a time when a customer asked me to sponsor an event they were hosting. The ask came with pressure; my main contact was responsible for bringing in sponsorship dollars, and it was clear this request had become tied to how they measured our partnership. The only problem?

I had zero budget available for sponsorships. I was stuck, feeling like my relationship might take a hit, and unsure how to proceed.

Finally, I asked a teammate, "How would you handle this?" Their answer was simple but game-changing: *"Just ask marketing. They should have a budget for that."*

Sure enough, when I approached my marketing team with the request, I found that they *did* have a budget earmarked for this exact type of initiative. They were thrilled to support the opportunity, and I was able to deliver for my customer.

From my contact's perspective, I had come through with exactly what they needed. From my marketing team's perspective, I had helped them allocate funds as intended. It was a win-win, and it all started with a quick ask for help.

Whether it's support at a trade show, a creative workaround to a customer challenge, or simply a second opinion, asking for help isn't a weakness; it's a strength. You'll still be the one delivering the solution to your customer, and they'll see you as a creative and dependable partner.

Meanwhile, your team will appreciate that you're resourceful enough to make use of the tools and people around you. Just be ready to return the favor.

One day, someone on your team may need your perspective, your experience, or your connections to help solve their customer's problem. The most effective account managers not only ask for help, they offer it, too.

Key 4 – Go Above and Beyond

Creativity often lives in the extra effort. When you're willing to go further than expected, you unlock opportunities others miss.

- Invest extra time to build the right resource or tailor the right pitch.
- Find a new way to present information that makes it clearer, faster, or more engaging.
- Solve problems before the customer even has to ask.

I once stayed late to build a custom dashboard for a client that no one else wanted to touch. It wasn't attention-grabbing, but it showed we were listening, and it won the deal.

That small effort paid off and taught me a valuable lesson. Creative account managers don't just imagine clever ideas; they execute them. And execution often requires more time, more energy, and more care than most people are willing to give. That's what makes it memorable.

Going above and beyond doesn't mean overworking yourself on every task. It means recognizing key moments when extra effort could make a big difference and rising to meet them.

Ultimately, customers remember who showed up, who put in the work, and who made it easier for them to succeed. Creativity paired with effort is what sets you apart.

Creative account managers go beyond thinking differently; they act differently, too. They explore new angles, reuse old ideas in innovative ways, invite others into the process, and push the boundaries a little further than expected.

Creativity isn't about being clever. It's about being resourceful, thoughtful, and willing to try something new to help your customer win.

Final Thought

Together, flexibility and creativity form a powerful duo that will elevate your account management success. Flexibility helps you adjust when plans change, while creativity helps you overcome challenges and turn them into opportunities.

Creativity without flexibility is wasted potential. Flexibility without creativity is reactive, not strategic. In a role built on relationships, being adaptable and imaginative isn't a bonus; it's a requirement.

Chapter 15 Recap

Key Takeaways

- Flexibility helps you respond in the moment. Creativity helps you reimagine what's possible.
- Letting go of your original plan isn't failure, it's progress.
- Success in account management requires you to pivot, rethink, and improvise as needed.

Reflection Questions

- Are you open to other people's ideas, or do you insist on doing things your way?
- When's the last time you solved a customer problem in an unconventional way?
- Where are you most resistant to changing your approach and why?

Apply It Now

- This week, say "yes" to someone's idea that is different than your own. See if it works.
- Identify a customer problem that's been hard to crack. Ask someone for a fresh take or brainstorm a bold new way to solve it.

Chapter 16

Rapid Learning and Resourcefulness

In account management, two of the most valuable and tightly linked skills are rapid learning and resourcefulness. Knowledge only becomes power when you're eager to learn and relentless about tracking down answers. One helps you absorb information fast. The other helps you apply it without delay. Together, they're a force multiplier.

I once had a customer ask for proof that our program was saving them money. Not just a general statement or rough estimate; they wanted a detailed report, broken down by month, with year-over-year comparisons and unit-level pricing deltas.

I knew the data existed. I knew it told a good story. What I didn't know was how to build the exact report they needed.

I had a basic understanding of Excel, but it wasn't enough to accomplish what was required. Pivot tables, lookup formulas, and conditional logic — I was out of my depth. But instead of handing it off or kicking the can down the road, I decided to figure it out.

I blocked off my afternoon, pulled up a few tutorials, and taught myself the formulas and formatting I needed. The next morning, I delivered a clean, intuitive report that made the savings story crystal clear.

The customer replied, *"This is exactly what we needed. Thank you! This will make it easy to show the value of our partnership to my leadership."*

That experience reminded me: You don't always need to have the answer, but you do need the willingness to learn it. And when you can pair speed with problem-solving, you become someone your customer can count on.

Whether you're explaining a product feature, solving a logistics hiccup, or navigating a complex renewal, your ability to learn quickly and find the right solution can make or break a deal.

Some of your best learning opportunities come directly from customers. When they ask about something you don't know or mention a need you hadn't considered, treat it like the start of a breadcrumb trail.

You don't need to be a subject-matter expert on day one. But you do need to learn fast, dig deep, and stay resourceful. These two skills will define your confidence in meetings, your credibility with customers, and your growth as a professional.

Let's dig into the keys that will help you build these essential skills.

– A Crash Course in Rapid Learning –

In account management, you're constantly faced with new information: products, processes, customers, industries. The key isn't knowing everything; it's learning fast. Rapid learning helps you close knowledge gaps before they become credibility gaps. The tips that follow will help you absorb information quickly, apply it with confidence, and become the go-to person your customers can count on.

Key 1 – Recognize the Value of Rapid Learning

The first step to becoming a faster learner is recognizing that knowledge is more than a nice-to-have; it's one of your most powerful assets. Every concept, insight, or workflow you master becomes part of your permanent toolkit, ready to be used again and again. Especially in account management, where your effectiveness depends on how well you understand not just your product, but your customer's world.

You don't need to be the expert in the room, but you do need to:

- Learn quickly and apply confidently.
- Close knowledge gaps before they become credibility gaps.
- Use each new learning as a way to improve how you show up.

When I first transitioned into a new role managing a major retail account, I quickly realized I was in over my head on one topic: supply chain logistics.

I had worked plenty of deals before, but this was the first time success depended on understanding how distribution centers, lead times, freight windows, and inventory replenishment actually worked.

During my first meeting with the customer, I was bombarded with questions like, *"Can you confirm if this ships FOB origin or FOB destination?"* and *"What's your replenishment cadence on seasonal items?"* I nodded, jotted notes, and barely bluffed my way through the conversation. In reality, I didn't even know what FOB stood for.

I left that meeting with one clear thought: If I don't figure this out fast, I'm going to be out of a job.

So that afternoon, I skipped lunch and went all in. I scoured internal documents, asked a teammate to walk me through the basics, and watched YouTube explainers on retail logistics. By the next meeting, I wasn't an expert, but I knew enough to answer questions with confidence.

That experience changed everything. I realized:

- Rapid learning isn't about surviving tough situations; it's a competitive edge.
- Understanding the backend helped me anticipate problems and provide more effective solutions.
- My customer noticed and trusted me more because of it.

The bottom line? Customers don't expect you to know everything on day one. But they do expect you to learn fast. And the faster you learn, the more valuable you become.

Key 2 - Use All Available Tools

We live in a golden age of information. Great account managers know how to use every tool at their disposal to solve problems and answer questions quickly and accurately. These tools include:

- **Google:** Ask it specific, thoughtful questions. But be sure to skip past the sponsored fluff.
- **ChatGPT and other AI tools:** Great for simplifying complex topics or pressure-testing your pitch.
- **Internal docs and wikis:** A goldmine, if you actually open them.

- **Your coworkers:** The best shortcuts usually come from someone who's done it before.

A few years back, I was remodeling my basement. I ran into a challenge I hadn't seen before: floating walls. I had never heard of them until I started researching, but in Colorado (where I live), shifting soil makes this unique construction method a necessity for basement walls. Within minutes, I had Googled the concept, found videos on YouTube, and learned how to build them. That's the world we live in. Almost anything you want to learn is a few clicks away.

The same principle applies to your work as an account manager. Don't sit around waiting for formal training. Instead, identify what you need to know, seek out sources of information, and block time to learn it.

If you can't find what you need online or in internal resources, look for industry classes or even ask your manager to point you toward helpful materials. The more proactive you are, the faster you'll close your knowledge gaps.

Key 3 – Learn to Search Smarter

Finding answers isn't just about trying harder; it's about searching smarter. Be specific, strategic, and structured. When searching:

- Start with your most unique keyword (e.g., "drop-ship compliance policy") and refine.

- Use quotation marks for exact phrases.
- Trim fluff. Avoid "the," "it," "thing," etc.
- Add qualifiers: "2024 pricing strategy" vs. just "pricing."
- Use domain filters: site:yourcompany.com or site:gov.

Smarter searches deliver faster, more relevant answers. The better you search, the faster you can show up prepared, credible, and confident — and your customers will notice.

> **Pro Tip: Build a Search Muscle**
>
> Don't wait until you're under pressure to start refining your search skills. Make a habit of experimenting with search operators, filters, and phrasing in your day-to-day work. The more reps you put in now, the faster and sharper you'll be when it counts. A well-crafted search can save you hours and sometimes even save a deal.

Rapid learning isn't about knowing everything; it's about knowing how to figure things out. The faster you can absorb new information, connect the dots, and apply it in real conversations, the more trust you'll earn. Customers respect curiosity when it leads to competence. Make learning your habit, and your confidence — and impact — will follow.

– A Crash Course in Being Resourceful –

Resourcefulness is what turns limited information into smart action. It's not about knowing everything; it's about knowing how to find what you need, who to ask, and how to keep moving when the answers aren't obvious.

Key 1 – Ask the Right People the Right Way

Some answers live in documents. Others live in people's heads. Great account managers know how to tap into both. Build a network of go-to experts, and ask questions clearly, respectfully, and with context.

Don't limit your search to formal documentation; look for tribal knowledge and tricks of the trade, the kind of insights that rarely show up in training decks but often make all the difference.

They're the shortcuts and insights that only come from real-world experience. Ask targeted questions like:

- "Have you handled this situation before?"
- "How would you explain this to a customer?"

- "Is there a resource that walks through this step-by-step?"

And don't stop at your immediate team, reach across departments. Many answers are only one Slack message or quick call away.

Key 2 – Always Verify Before You Share

Speed is good, but accuracy wins trust. One wrong answer travels faster than ten right ones. Verify everything before it hits the customer's inbox. Before you pass along information:

- Check the source and publication date.
- Look for confirmation in a second location (or person).
- If you're unsure, say: "Let me confirm before I finalize that for you."

That sentence can save you from losing credibility.

Pro Tip: Build Your Personal Answer Bank

Start saving links, internal contacts, helpful documents, and go-to phrases for the questions you hear most often. This living resource will help you respond more quickly and confidently without relying solely on memory.

Key 3 – Cultivate Curiosity

Curiosity is the difference between average account managers and exceptional ones. When you're curious, you don't wait to be told what matters; you go out and look for it. And often, that curiosity leads directly to opportunities. If you want to grow your influence, customer base, or career, your ability to learn fast is your biggest lever.

I once had a mid-sized customer who always seemed a bit disengaged during check-ins. We had consistent orders, but no growth. One day, in an offhand comment, they mentioned how frustrating it was that their sales team couldn't customize marketing materials. That wasn't something they'd ever flagged as a formal need, but it sparked my curiosity.

I dug into our internal tools and found a beta feature that allowed localized asset customization. I asked my marketing team for access, tested it myself, and then brought a short demo to our next meeting.

Their eyes lit up. That small feature solved a real problem, and it led to a bigger conversation about how we could support their sales enablement across the board. Within two months, they tripled their spend with us.

The key? I didn't wait for them to ask for a solution. I let curiosity guide me to it.

Resourceful account managers don't freeze when they hit a wall; they find another way through. Whether it's asking the right person, checking one more source, or uncovering a tool no one's using, they stay curious and keep moving. The answers are out there. Your job is to track them down and put them to work.

Final Thought

Customers don't expect perfection, but they do respect hustle. When you learn fast, ask thoughtful questions, and track down what others miss, you become the partner they trust most. Rapid learning and resourcefulness are more than helpful skills, they're your edge.

Chapter 16 Recap

Key Takeaways

- Rapid learning and resourcefulness are two of the most valuable account management skills.
- You don't need to have every answer, but you need to have the confidence and skill to find them.
- Curiosity, proactivity, and verification build long-term credibility with customers.

Reflection Questions

- When was the last time you learned something that changed how you approached a customer?
- When you're stumped, do you guess, delay, or dig in to find the answer?

Apply It Now

- Schedule 30 minutes this week to learn about a feature, product, or trend you've been avoiding.
- Build your personal "answer bank." Save links, contacts, or summaries of the 10 most common questions you get asked.

Chapter 17

Understanding and Using Metrics

Early in my career, I walked into a quarterly review with my customer feeling confident. The relationship was strong, and I knew we'd helped improve some key processes. But halfway through the meeting, he asked, *"Do you know how much we've actually saved since switching to your program?"*

I stumbled. I had anecdotal wins and general improvements to point to, but no hard numbers. I hadn't quantified the savings, let alone framed them in a way that would hold up under scrutiny. The meeting limped to the finish line, and while nothing broke, I knew I'd missed a chance to reinforce our value. It was a painful but important realization: good relationships get you in the room, but data earns you a seat at the table. Without it, even your best efforts can be undervalued or overlooked.

After that, I made it a rule: never show up to a review without a metric that matters. I built a simple template to estimate savings based on common inputs. And before every major meeting, I made sure I had at least one data-backed takeaway tied to results.

By the next review, I was ready, and this time, the savings story led the conversation instead of stalling it.

Account managers often operate behind the scenes, building relationships, resolving problems, and ensuring that things run smoothly. However, while the work may appear "soft" on the surface, its impact is anything but. In reality, great account managers are deeply tied to results. And in business, results are measured in metrics.

When used correctly, metrics do more than validate your performance; they help you see around corners, prioritize your time, and strengthen your credibility. They allow you to anticipate churn, justify expansion, and hold your own in cross-functional meetings with operations, marketing, or finance.

This chapter isn't about turning you into a spreadsheet expert or a data analyst. It's about helping you master the language of value so you can tell compelling stories, drive smart decisions, and grow your career with confidence.

– A Crash Course in Understanding and Using Metrics –

Metrics can feel overwhelming, especially if you're not a numbers person. But they don't have to be. Once you know what to look for and how to use it, data becomes one of your most powerful tools.

Metrics are more than charts and dashboards. They let you see clearly, act decisively, and prove your impact. This crash course will help you turn numbers into knowledge, and knowledge into influence.

Key 1 – Recognize The Value of Metrics

Account managers may not close deals every day, but they are still in a performance role. The ability to read, interpret, and use metrics separates reactive account managers from strategic ones. Metrics help you:

- Track account health over time.
- Flag risks before they turn into problems.
- Spot growth opportunities as they emerge.
- Quantify your impact on the business.
- Tell your own story before someone else tells it.

Metrics provide clarity and credibility. They don't just show what's happening; they reveal why, and what you should do next. If you want a promotion, a raise, or a shot at a bigger book, you'll need to prove performance. Metrics give you the proof.

Key 2 – Understand the Core Categories

Metrics can feel overwhelming until you realize most of what matters falls into five core buckets. Master these, and you'll be ahead of 90% of your peers.

1. Revenue Metrics

These show what your account is worth and how it's performing.

- Book size
- Year-over-year growth
- Net new vs. renewal vs. upsell
- Recurring vs. project-based revenue
- Forecast vs. actuals

Revenue is the scoreboard. Know where you're winning and where you're vulnerable.

2. Engagement Metrics

These reveal how connected you are to your customers.

- Meeting frequency and attendance
- Access to decision-makers
- Email responsiveness

- Participation in business reviews

Engagement drops before revenue does. Watch these closely.

3. Customer Sentiment

This is the "gut feel" made measurable.

- Customer Satisfaction, Net Promoter, or other survey scores
- Language shifts ("We're reevaluating budgets...")
- Reactions in meetings, tone in emails

Customers often signal frustration long before they escalate or churn.

4. Support and Issue Trends

This helps you track friction and delivery issues.

- Ticket volume or escalation rate
- Recurring complaints or Service Level Agreement misses
- Resolution speed and satisfaction

Even when the product performs well, friction, such as delivery delays, long response times, or unclear processes, can quietly erode trust.

5. Internal Performance Metrics

These reflect how your organization sees you.

- CRM hygiene (activity logging, forecast accuracy)

- Internal responsiveness (to support, product, leadership)
- Participation in cross-functional initiatives

Internal reputation matters. Want better resources or visibility? Hit your metrics.

Key 3 – Using Metrics to Drive Strategy

Metrics aren't just for monthly reports; they should shape your day-to-day priorities. Ask yourself:

- Which accounts are slipping in engagement or revenue?
- Which customers are showing signs of readiness to grow?
- Where do I need to proactively intervene?
- What can I use to support my gut instinct with hard data?

I once had an account that went quiet: no emails, no orders, no meetings. Instead of assuming they were just busy, I looked at the data: their volume had dropped by 40% in two months, and support tickets were up.

I got hold of my main contact by phone and confirmed that they were shopping competitors. My early outreach gave me just enough time to address the issues and preserve the business.

When you review your book regularly through the lens of engagement, support, and revenue, you stop reacting to problems and start preventing them.

> **Pro Tip: Let the Data Speak First**
>
> Don't wait for trouble to become obvious. Use metrics to spot red flags early, confirm your instincts, and guide where to focus. The sooner you act on the signals, the more control you have over the outcome.

Key 4 - Communicate Your Metrics Like a Pro

Knowing your metrics isn't enough. You have to use them to influence others.

Internally:
- Keep reporting clean and structured.
- Focus on what changed, why, and what you're doing about it.
- Use visuals when possible (charts, graphs, summaries).
- Don't just say "everything's fine." Prove it.

With customers:
- Use scorecards or dashboards in business reviews and renewal meetings.
- Highlight improvements: support down, usage up, outcomes achieved.
- Frame metrics in terms of customer value, not internal KPIs. Instead of saying, "Support volume dropped 30%," say, "We reduced friction for your team, which means less downtime and fewer headaches."

The ability to tell a metrics-backed story in a customer meeting or internal review earns you credibility fast. It's one of the highest-impact skills you can develop.

Key 5 – Focus on the Right Metrics

You can't track everything. And you don't need to.

Pick 3–5 key metrics that reflect real account health signals. For me, it's:

- Sales vs. forecast
- Engagement frequency
- Support volume

Track them. Spot trends. Take action.

Every Monday, I review those metrics across my book. If something's off, I make that my priority. It's a 10-minute ritual that saves me hours later.

Avoid these two traps:

- **Data overload:** You're drowning in dashboards but not taking action.
- **Data denial:** You go by gut, but you're missing silent signals.

Find the middle ground: meaningful metrics, reviewed regularly, acted on deliberately.

Key 6 – Metrics Are Career Currency

Metrics don't only tell you how your accounts are doing; they tell others how *you* are doing.

In performance reviews, promotions, and team meetings, you'll often be asked:

- How's your book of business performing?
- What's working? What's not?
- Where should we invest more?

If you have the metrics, you'll shine. If you don't, you'll stall.

Frame your metrics for career growth:

- "I grew my book by 18% YoY with a 92% renewal rate."

- "I reduced support volume by 40% through process fixes."
- "I led quarterly business review meetings with 90% of my top accounts this quarter."

That's not bragging, it's business fluency. It shows that you understand not just what you did, but why it mattered.

Metrics aren't there to be checked off a list; they're tools to drive action. When you track the right numbers, interpret them with intention, and apply what you learn, you shift from reactive to strategic. Great account managers don't watch the data from the sidelines; they use it to lead.

Final Thought

Metrics turn the invisible into the undeniable. They help you see what's working, spot what's changing, and prove the value you deliver. Whether you're advocating for a customer, preparing for a business review, or making a case for your own promotion, data is your ally.

But metrics aren't powerful on their own. They become powerful when *you* use them with clarity, purpose, and confidence. Master the numbers, and you'll master the narrative.

Chapter 17 Recap

Key Takeaways

- Metrics are not an optional add-on; they're how account managers measure and prove their value.
- Learn which numbers matter, track them consistently, and use them to drive decisions.
- Use metrics to influence your customers, inform your team, and guide your own career.

Reflection Questions

- What metrics do you track regularly? Are they the right ones?
- Can you clearly explain your account performance to your manager today?
- Are you using data to drive action or just to report the past?

Apply It Now

- Pick one at-risk and one healthy account. Pull their key metrics side by side. What patterns emerge?
- Create a simple weekly dashboard for yourself. Track 3–5 core KPIs across all accounts.

Chapter 18

Putting it All Together

You've spent this book sharpening the skills that define great B2B account managers; now it's time to bring them together. Each skill stands on its own, but your success as an account manager doesn't come from mastering any single one. It comes from putting them all together. Knowing *when* to use each skill and *how* to blend them fluidly in the real world.

Think about it this way: being great at presenting won't matter if you never follow through. Building strong relationships won't translate to long-term value if you can't understand and act on what the metrics are telling you. And even the best communicator will struggle if they're not genuinely listening. These skills are not individual tools; they're parts of a larger system. To succeed in this role, you need to bring them together into a cohesive, repeatable approach to account management.

And here's the truth: putting it all together is a skill in and of itself. It can't be learned just by reading (even this book). You have to practice. You have to apply what you've learned. The good news? You don't need a job title to do that.

Account Management Is Everywhere

Whether you're still in school, working in a different role, or actively managing a book of business, you already have opportunities to practice. Account management is about long-term influence and value creation, and the chance to practice those skills exists all around you.

- **In school**: Building rapport with classmates and teachers is practice in relationship-building. Coordinating a group project? That's stakeholder management. Pitching your idea for how to divide the workload? That's presenting.
- **At home**: Negotiating where to eat or how to split chores? That's pitching. Following up on a shared task? That's follow-through. Listening to your spouse's frustration and adjusting your approach? That's customer obsession.
- **In any job**: You don't need to carry a sales quota to practice these skills. Showing up prepared, listening to your manager, managing internal projects, or asking

smart questions all reinforce the same muscles you'll use in an account manager role.

Wherever you are, every conversation is an opportunity to practice. Start blending the skills now, and when you do land that account management role, you'll already be ahead of the curve.

Long-Term Relationships Are the Goal

No matter how complex the job gets, your focus as an account manager remains simple: build and maintain fruitful, long-term relationships with your customers. That means playing the long game, even when short-term opportunities are tempting.

There will be times when a quick sale is within reach, but the pitch could damage trust or jeopardize future opportunities. In those moments, you'll need to pause and ask yourself: "Is this sale worth jeopardizing the relationship I've spent months or years building?"

More often than not, it's better to walk away from the short-term win in favor of protecting the long-term partnership. Your success depends not on how many products you sell this quarter, but on how often your customer chooses you over the alternatives, quarter after quarter.

Never a Boring Day

The best part of account management is that no two days are the same. You'll wear a dozen hats, sometimes all in the same week.

- One day, you're solving a delivery issue or chasing down a late invoice.
- The next day, you're learning the ins and outs of a new product feature and prepping a pitch.
- Then, you're in front of an executive team, presenting a roadmap and securing buy-in.
- Later, you're smoothing over tension between your internal ops team and your customer's support lead.

And on some days, you'll just be connecting, deepening the relationship without a formal agenda, making sure your customer feels heard, seen, and valued.

It's a demanding job. But it's also incredibly rewarding. You'll build relationships that last beyond the role. You'll develop skills that translate to almost any career. And you'll play a key role in driving real results for your company and your customers.

Not for Everyone, But It Can Be for You

B2B account management isn't easy. It's not always glamorous. Some days, it'll test your patience, your resilience, and your ability to navigate ambiguity. But if you've made it through this book, and more importantly, if you're willing to apply what you've learned, then this career might just be the right one for you.

You don't have to be born with a certain personality type. You don't need a specific degree or a sales pedigree. You just need to:

- Learn the core skills of the role.
- Dedicate time to mastering them.
- Practice them at every opportunity.
- And above all, prioritize the customer and the long-term relationship.

If you can do that — and you absolutely can — you'll be successful in this role. You'll be great at it.

If you're wondering what all of this looks like in real life, here's a story that brings it all together.

A Story About Putting It All Together

There's one story that stands out in my mind because it forced me to use almost every skill in the account management toolkit. It's the perfect example of what this job really looks like when done right.

It began with a familiar red flag: an email from my customer saying they were "reviewing their options" ahead of their renewal. In account management, that's code for: *"We're shopping around."* I wasn't surprised. Engagement had been dipping. We were having fewer meetings, their responses had gotten slower, and now the risk was real.

The pressure was high. This was a key account, and the renewal was a major part of my book. My gut instinct was to go straight into pitch mode and start selling. But I paused. I reminded myself: this is exactly where good account managers don't sell; they listen. So, I scheduled a call, opened it with zero pressure, and simply asked:

"Can you help me understand what's driving this review?"

Then I stopped talking and let them fill the silence.

What I learned changed everything. Yes, a competitor had come in with a lower price, but that wasn't the real problem. Their deeper concern was trust. Several support issues in the past quarter had shaken their confidence in our ability to deliver. I hadn't fully realized the impact those issues had until I listened to my customer describe the experience from their perspective.

Now that I understood the concern, I turned to metrics. I pulled reports on support ticket volume, resolution times, platform usage, and order consistency. The data told a clearer story: yes, there had been a spike in support cases, but they were all tied to the rollout of a new product that was now complete. More importantly, the customer's usage data was trending up, showing that despite the hiccups, our product was still delivering real value.

Armed with that data, I started thinking creatively. Rather than reacting with a discount, like the competitor had done, I proposed something different: a dedicated support escalation plan. It included named contacts during critical periods and proactive quarterly check-ins to ensure alignment. This solution addressed the real issue — trust — without sacrificing margin.

But ideas only matter if they can be executed. So I got to work on internal selling. I rallied our support and operations teams, built a case for why this account mattered, and earned their buy-in to support the plan. At the same time, I followed up with the customer consistently with clear communication. No dropped balls, no radio silence.

By the time we sat down for the renewal meeting, we weren't having a pricing conversation; we were having a partnership conversation. I walked them through the data, acknowledged the past challenges, presented the support plan, and showed them the road ahead. I used everything: presenting, pitching, objection handling, storytelling, metrics, creativity, internal alignment, and follow-through.

And it worked.

They renewed. More than that, they expanded the partnership six months later.

The lesson? No one skill saved the deal. It was the combination that made the difference.

- **Listening** revealed the real issue.
- **Metrics** gave me the proof.
- **Creativity** delivered a tailored solution.
- **Internal selling** made it possible.
- **Follow-through** earned back trust.
- And the **pitch** tied it all together.

That's what putting it all together looks like. And it's how great account managers win.

What It Taught Me

That renewal didn't just save the account; it changed how I saw the role.

Before that moment, I thought success in account management meant being the most prepared, the most persuasive, the person with all the answers. But I learned that it's not about perfection. It's about presence. About listening fully, responding honestly, and showing your customer that you're in it with them; not just for the sale, but for the long haul.

That realization changed everything. It made me a better partner to my customers. A better teammate. A better professional. And it's why I believe this role is one of the most rewarding in business. Not because of the titles or target earnings, but because of the growth it demands and the trust it builds.

Final Thought

You've made it to the end, but in truth, this isn't the end at all. What you have in your hands is a playbook, not a textbook. These aren't just tips and tricks; they're the tools of a trusted advisor, a problem solver, and a partner customers rely on.

You won't master everything in one day, and you don't have to. Success in account management isn't about perfection. It's about progress. About showing up prepared, being relentlessly curious, leading with empathy, and always adding value.

Your customers are counting on someone who knows how to think like a partner, not just a vendor. You're that person now. So go sharpen your skills, trust your instincts, lean into the hard conversations, and lead every relationship forward.

You already know how to communicate, listen, present, and follow through. Now you know how to put it all together.

The next chapter belongs to you.

Chapter 18 Recap

Key Takeaways

- Great account managers don't just master individual skills; they know how to use them in combination.
- You don't need a formal job to start practicing account management. Opportunities exist all around you.
- Long-term relationships, not short-term wins, are the foundation of sustained success.

Reflection Questions

- Which skills from this book come naturally to you? Which ones do you need to consciously work on?
- Can you think of a recent interaction at work, home, or school, where applying multiple skills could have improved the outcome?

Apply It Now

- Pick a real-world situation, personal or professional, and deliberately apply at least three different skills from this book.
- Reflect on the result. What worked? What surprised you? What would you do differently next time?

Glossary of Account Management Terms

A guide to the key terms used throughout this book. Whether you're new to B2B account management or just want to sharpen your understanding, these definitions serve as a quick reference.

Core Terms

Account Management – A relationship-based sales role focused on long-term value, retention, and growth between two businesses, rather than one-time transactions.

Account Manager – A professional responsible for building trust, solving problems, and serving as the main point of contact between two companies.

B2B (Business-to-Business) – Transactions or relationships between two companies, such as a software provider selling to a retailer.

B2C (Business-to-Consumer) – Transactions between a business and an individual consumer, such as a retail store selling directly to a shopper.

One-Time Salesperson – A sales role focused on closing a transaction without an ongoing relationship. The goal is typically a quick, one-off sale.

Customer Obsession – A mindset that prioritizes understanding and delivering what's best for the customer, even when it requires extra effort or creativity.

Communication Styles

Email Communication – Written correspondence, often asynchronous. Common formats include meeting recaps, follow-ups, and outreach.

- **Cold Email** – Outreach to someone you don't know and who isn't expecting to hear from you.
- **Warm Email** – Outreach to someone you know or who is expecting contact.
- **Internal Email** – Communication with colleagues within your company.
- **External Email** – Communication with contacts outside your organization, like customers or partners.

Verbal Communication – Spoken communication, including phone calls, virtual meetings, or in-person discussions. Often used when nuance, tone, or trust-building is critical.

Meeting Formats

In-Person Meeting – A face-to-face meeting, usually at the customer's office or a neutral site. Useful for building trust and gaining deeper insights.

Virtual Meeting – A meeting that happens over a video conferencing platform like Zoom or Microsoft Teams.

Phone Call – A voice-only verbal exchange, often quicker and less formal than video meetings.

One-to-One Meeting – A meeting between one representative from your company and one from the customer's. Ideal for relationship-building and personalized discussion.

Small Group Meeting – A meeting with 2–5 stakeholders from the customer side. Typically used for business reviews or collaborative planning.

One-to-Many Meeting – A presentation-style format where you're delivering a message to a larger group, such as a training, demo, or event.

- **Main Stage Presentation** – A high-stakes, large-audience presentation, such as a keynote or conference talk. Typically formal and highly structured.

- **Round-Robin Meeting** – A series of short, repeat presentations delivered to multiple groups in succession, often at events.
- **Trade Show Booth Meeting** – Informal, rapid-fire engagements at industry events, where you share short pitches or demos as people visit your booth.

Tools and Techniques

Deck – A slide-based presentation, typically created in PowerPoint, Keynote, or Google Slides. Used during meetings to support your message visually.

Objection – A statement or question from a customer that challenges your proposal or disrupts your intended direction.

Pitch – A structured way of presenting your product, idea, or solution to persuade the audience or spark interest.

Internal Selling – Advocating within your own organization to get support, resources, or buy-in needed to deliver for your customers.

Multi-Threading – Building relationships with multiple contacts at a customer's organization to strengthen influence and reduce risk. Just be sure to keep your main contact looped in and positioned as your lead.

Performance and Metrics

Metrics – Quantitative data used to evaluate account health, performance, or customer satisfaction. Used to inform decisions and guide strategy.

Key types of metrics:

- **Revenue Metrics** – Indicators of account size and performance (e.g., growth, renewals, forecast).
- **Engagement Metrics** – Measures of customer activity and involvement (e.g., meeting frequency, responsiveness).
- **Customer Sentiment** – Perceived satisfaction and tone of the relationship (e.g., survey scores, feedback).
- **Support and Issue Trends** – Service-related indicators (e.g., ticket volume, resolution speed).
- **Internal Performance Metrics** – Measures of how you're viewed within your organization (e.g., CRM hygiene, forecast accuracy).

CRM (Customer Relationship Management) – Software used to track customer interactions, manage pipelines, and log account activities.

ABOUT THE AUTHOR

Bill Senese is a seasoned B2B account manager with a career spanning from local startups to global brands. He began his journey in 2010 as an Account Executive at a small insurance marketing firm and has since led teams, managed national accounts, and built a reputation for driving results and fostering lasting customer relationships. Today, he serves as a Senior Strategic Adoption Manager for one of the world's most recognized brands.

Born in the south suburbs of Chicago, Bill studied Physical Education at Eastern Illinois University before earning his MBA from the University of Colorado. A passionate mentor and coach, he now gives back to the profession through thought leadership, training, and advocacy for raising talent in account management.

Outside of work, Bill is a husband, a father of two, a record-setting masters swimmer, and a serial hobbyist. Whether he's cheering on his kids, helping his wife chase her goal of running a marathon in every state, or diving into his next DIY project or novel, Bill brings the same energy and curiosity to life that he brings to his career.

Sleep? He'll get to that eventually.

COMING SOON!

WWW.YOUTUBE.COM/@THESHOWONTHAT

Want more? Watch *The Show on That*

Your companion to *The Book on That*, *The Show on That* brings B2B account management to life. Tune in for chapter deep dives, real-world breakdowns, and exclusive interviews with veteran account managers. Practical insights, fresh perspectives — all in one place.

Subscribe on YouTube and keep learning.

www.ingramcontent.com/pod-product-compliance
Lightning Source LLC
Chambersburg PA
CBHW021146160426
43194CB00007B/704